These Men
SHALL NEVER DIE

These Men
SHALL NEVER DIE

☆ ☆ ☆ ☆ ☆ ☆ ☆ ☆ ☆ ☆ ☆ ☆ ☆

By

LOWELL THOMAS

Illustrated with OFFICIAL PHOTOGRAPHS *by*
U. S. ARMY AIR CORPS
U. S. ARMY SIGNAL CORPS
U. S. NAVY
U. S. MARINE CORPS

Essay Index Reprint Series

BOOKS FOR LIBRARIES PRESS
FREEPORT, NEW YORK

D736
T455
1971

INTERNATIONAL STANDARD BOOK NUMBER:
0-8369-2379-0

LIBRARY OF CONGRESS CATALOG CARD NUMBER:
73-152217

PRINTED IN THE UNITED STATES OF AMERICA

This book is dedicated to those American fighting men whose stories have not been included in this volume, but should have been.

A BATTALION OF THE BRAVE

To a newsman, one of the vivid things about America at war is the daily quota of hero stories from our forces that flash in the distant war zones. When you are in close touch with the news wire daily, you have a closer view of the abundant accounts of individual courage and wealth of bravery. To me it has been simply dazzling.

The news gives us glowing accounts of heroic deeds, but these are a fraction only of the whole. Many magnificent exploits are headlined, while many more are mentioned only briefly—if at all. Daily reports tell of decorations with citations conferred on fighting men who have distinguished themselves. These citations often tell little of the circumstances incident to a hero's valorous deed. Yet behind the laconic words of each citation lies a blazing story of war and peril.

Military secrecy requires many a story to be withheld in whole or in part for the time being. Often communications in a theater of action are too busy to transmit the drama of the ever-occurring episodes. Many great stories never get into the news, and many that do are only partly related, with much left unexplained.

Of course, the inspiring record should be made known, so that it may be read to be realized. The purpose of this book is to give some hint of the glory of individual courage that has been only partly disclosed to us: in many cases not disclosed at all.

A selection has been made of representative men of valor who have been honored during America's first year of war. They are typical of many another equally distinguished, the plan being to present a cross-section of heroism so abundantly displayed by the fighting men of this nation. A picture of American youth is given, a new interpretation of the young generation of this land: American youth in war. We see the flaming spirit of lads who have gone from cities, small towns, and farms, your neighborhood and mine. They have the preponderant place on the roll call of the decorated.

The men whose stories are told have been selected by *competent military judgment*, the kind of judgment that awards the decorations and citations of war. The Army, the Navy, and the Marine Corps are schools of courage, and their higher officers are skilled and experienced in estimating the hardihood of the human spirit.

"They were fighting virtually with their bare hands," an officer told me. "They were short of weapons, short of ammunition, short of medical supplies, short of food. Their air support was a mere fraction of what they needed. The flying force was short of planes, short of armament, short of spare parts, short of flying fields, short of everything in the way of the elaborate equipment that is needed for air power. The cry was, 'Send us something!' They were pleading, begging, as they fought with their backs against the wall."

That drastic statement applies in general to the Americans at the fighting fronts during the first year of the war. This nation was taken by surprise, was caught unprepared. It had no giant masses of equipment then, no stupendous power of guns, no swarms of tanks, no clouds of planes. During that first year, America, now the world's master producer of armament, had to depend on the raw courage of naked American flesh—the mere heart of its fighting men. It had to wage a desperate last-ditch battle against superior forces that were supplied abundantly with every sort of armament. These men stood against heartbreaking odds, outnumbered and outgunned.

We shall not likely see that brand of courage again which was displayed so abundantly during America's first year at war. Valor there will be, rich surpluses of the American fighting spirit flaming in men well-armed and well-equipped. These will not have to endure the ordeal of the men of the first year, who on many battlefronts held and pushed back the enemy virtually with bare hands.

In gathering this material I had occasion to make some personal contacts that revealed vivid hints of the personalities of the men whose stories are to be told. They present sharp contrasts, running a wide range of human nature.

I went to a quiet homelike apartment in upper Manhattan, and talked with the parents of Lieutenant John James Powers who gave his life in a South Pacific dive bomb attack against Japanese warships. Mr. and Mrs. Powers were like any other American parents: middle-aged, quiet, courteous, hospitable. They received me in the comfortable living room of a home they had occupied for many years. They told me little things about Lieutenant Powers, and the picture they drew might be taken as a sort of common denominator of fine American youth. The hero of sea and air battle had been much like any other first-rate son reared in an American home: sound, healthy, normal, a lover of sports and diligent at tasks.

Then take Lieutenant Alexander Nininger, Jr. who perished while doing a relentless job of killing Japs on Bataan. A fierce, hard-bitten soldier? No, not at all. G. H. Martin of Fort Lauderdale, Florida, knew Sandy Nininger well. He writes me that the future hero of Bataan was physically below the average. "In school Sandy went out for all athletic teams," the letter states, "and because of his inferiority, his presence was resented by his fellow students. He never complained when they deliberately stepped on his hands while he was trying to play end in football. He never resented it when they tried to discourage his presence on the field. By the time he was a senior he had developed into a fairly good end, enough to earn his letter."

Lieutenant Nininger's mother writes: "He was deeply religious, and a boy of gentle disposition. When he was about to enter upon his military career, somebody said to him: 'Sandy, you are so loving and gentle, you could not hate and fight and kill people, could you?' Sandy replied calmly: 'I couldn't have any hate in my heart for anyone, but I will fight our enemy out of love for my country, my home, and my church.' "

By way of contrast, there is Joe Foss who, in the South Pacific air war, established himself as the American ace of aces. Joe

Foss, when he returned to the United States to receive the Congressional Medal of Honor, impressed those who met him as the perfect fighting man, the instinctive and relentless hunter, the remorseless Jap-killer. Tall, handsome, modest, he is the embodiment of the frontiersman of old, the stalker of game, the trailer of human enemies.

I met Swede Larsen, who at Guadalcanal established himself as number-one aerial torpedo ace. Swede Larsen was cheery, light-hearted, "the happy warrior." He gave the impression that he didn't hate Japanese: didn't hate anybody. He simply enjoyed his job, reveling in the excitements and perils of a torpedo plane attack against a hostile ship. How much he enjoyed it was hinted by a thing he said. We are accustomed to regard Guadalcanal as a jungle hell hole. Swede Larsen remarked that, when the war was over, he'd like to go back to Guadalcanal.

In these stories I have tried to present the personalities of men of valor, as well as their exploits. Their names, their personalities, and their exploits compounded together may well be put into a single phrase: "These Men Shall Never Die."

Lowell Thomas

CONTENTS

CONTENTS

CONTENTS

THE ROLL CALL OF HEROES

PART ONE

PEARL HARBOR AND WAKE ISLAND

LIEUTENANT CLARENCE E. DICKINSON, JR., U.S.N., Raleigh, North Carolina.
Navy Cross
Gold Star in lieu of Second Navy Cross
Second Gold Star in lieu of Third Navy Cross

One of the most remarkable photographs of all time, the destroyer *Shaw* blowing up at Pearl Harbor, its magazine exploding. The *Shaw* was hit by a bomb from the fleet of Japanese planes, which outnumbered the sky force that American flyers, such as Lieutenant Dickinson, braved so boldly.

THE FIRST DEED OF VALOR

AS NEARLY as I can figure, the very first deed of valor in the war between the United States and Japan was performed by Lieutenant Clarence Earle Dickinson of Raleigh, North Carolina. He was piloting a plane, was in the air, when the oncoming Japanese air raiders struck at the fleet at Pearl Harbor. In a scout plane he was on an observation mission when the Japs swarmed through the air for their sneak punch of December 7.

That fateful morning Lieutenant Dickinson was doing dawn patrol. He, no more than any other American, had any notion that Japanese aircraft carriers had come through the night to within air-striking distance of Pearl Harbor. At the controls without a worry in the world, he saw squadrons of planes coming in from the sea. It must have been the dizziest of surprises to catch the first glimpse of the enemy sky fleet winging to deliver the treacherous blow.

Enemy fighters spotted the lone American and darted for a ganging attack. The battle was utterly unequal. The American was a mere scout plane meant for observation, and they were speedy killers of the sky. The lone aircraft fought back, but was overwhelmed by superior gun power. Dickinson's gunner was killed, and fire broke out. Dickinson continued to shoot, until the flames forced him out of the cockpit. He took to his parachute.

He was over land, came down safely, and made his way back to the Pearl Harbor Naval Air Station. There he heard of the incredible events that were occurring—the surprise bombing and torpedo plane attack on the fleet in Pearl Harbor, the ferocious and devastating assault of "the day that will live in infamy." Dickinson reported to his commanding officer—but kept a few things to himself. He said nothing about the harrowing ordeal of bullets and fire that he had gone through. He mentioned briefly the shooting down of his plane, skipping the details of fiery trial and blazing valor. He was afraid that, after such an experience, he would be kept on the ground. He wanted to carry on.

He took off again in another scout plane, and flew to gather information. In the climactic fury of the Japanese air attack, he made an observation air tour of one hundred and seventy-five miles, weaving among the enemy squadrons.

Such is the first story of individual American exploits in our war with Japan. It was typical of many another on that Pearl Harbor day of surprise and havoc, when in the turmoil of the unexpected assault men rose to heights of initiative and daring action. For Dickinson it was only a beginning. He went on to distinguish himself repeatedly, and it is a heartening thing to record that the first man on the hero list has since then doubled and redoubled his fame.

Three days after Pearl Harbor, flying a bomber, he attacked a Jap submarine on the surface. The Jap had antiaircraft guns, and blazed away with a hail of bullets, but Dickinson braved the fire contemptuously, and fought a battle of plane against sub. It was one of those fantastic things, contradicting elements at war, the sky versus the undersea. The antiaircraft guns of the low lying submarine had a fair target—Dickinson came down that low. He swooped virtually into the bullets to place his bombs effectively. Daring plus clever flying tactics won the victory.

In the American sea and air raid against the Gilbert and Marshall Islands, Dickinson was back on the observation job—flight officer of a scouting squadron that directed the gunfire of American warships against targets on shore. In a storm of antiaircraft fire and with Jap fighter planes attacking, Dickinson stuck doggedly to his target spotting. The directions that he signalled guided American naval shells for heavy hits on an important shore installation and a big ship. It takes strength of nerve to stay up there at a danger angle of the sky, enduring rather than fighting, being shot at with little opportunity to shoot, as in the case of Dickinson, offering himself as a target so that shells from the warships might find their targets.

He was at Midway, doing bombing work, and braved a climax of the peril of antiaircraft fire—one of the greatest concentrations of shells and bullets meant to destroy planes. It was a case of diving into a tempest of bullets and shells, with tracers streaking such a close pattern that it seemed as if no plane could live through them. Dickinson was among the foremost of the bombers that swooped down upon the Japs, smacking them with bombs and thwarting their grandiose plan for capturing Hawaii. His citation for that job states: "He boldly pressed home devastating attacks against the Japanese invasion fleet." How much could one flyer accomplish? How important could the work of one single bomber really be? Let's look at the citation again. It summarizes by saying that Dickinson "contributed in a large degree to the decisive victory of our forces."

After starting out as first on the list at Pearl Harbor, Dickinson continued so well that his record may be taken as presenting a full range of flying heroism in the Pacific war.

LIEUTENANT GEORGE S. WELCH, U.S.A., Wilmington, Delaware
Distinguished Service Cross
Lieutenant Welch was decorated by President Roosevelt at the White House on May 25
for shooting down four Japanese planes in the surprise attack on Pearl Harbor. The
War Department described the action as "magnificent fighting" and worthy of a
veteran fighter.

The destruction of the battleship *Arizona*, the victim of an incredibly lucky hit—an enemy bomb going down a smokestack and exploding the magazines. While the treacherous enemy was attacking ships in the harbor, Lieutenant Welch and his partner, Lieutenant Taylor, were shooting down one plane after another.

INK SCARCELY DRY

WHEN THE first wave of Japanese planes came over Pearl Harbor, Second Lieutenant George S. Welch was at Wheeler Field. Enemy bombers attacked the field. The Wilmington, Delaware lad was a new arrival in Hawaii. He had become a pilot only recently: "The ink on his commission was scarcely dry," as his citation states. And there he was, gaping up at Japanese bombers.

That fearful December 7 at Pearl Harbor, there was a tragic lot of bungling, bewilderment, and confusion. Why had the Japanese not been spotted as they came in? Why was Pearl

[7]

Harbor taken so utterly by surprise, when all the world knew that the peril of war was so great? These are questions that up to now have not been satisfactorily answered. What we can show here is that there were some who did not lose their heads, some who, in the face of the terrifyingly unexpected, kept their heads and did their jobs well: sometimes with dazzling heroism. One of these was George Welch, the lad who not long before had departed from his Delaware home to join the Air Force, and who was fresh and green from training school.

With him was his pal, Second Lieutenant Kenneth M. Taylor of Hominy, Oklahoma, he too, a youngster not long out of an American home. Their impulse was to leap to their planes and attack the enemy, but the planes of their squadron were not at Wheeler Field, but at Haleiwa, ten miles away. Kenneth Taylor had an automobile. The two jumped in and started to drive.

All the way to the squadron they were under attack, Japanese planes diving at the speeding automobile. At Haleiwa they found their own planes okay, although the Japanese were bombing aircraft on the ground far and wide. Welch and Taylor took off, and were only a thousand feet up when they spotted enemy planes, a dozen of them.

George Welch picked out a dive bomber, swooped down upon it, got into position to fire, and discovered this appalling fact: his plane was equipped with two 50-calibre machine guns and four 30-calibre guns. When he tried to fire the fifties—nothing doing: they had been disconnected. One of the 30-calibre guns failed to shoot. It jammed. That left George Welch with a fraction of normal fire power. Maybe he should have turned back to the flying field to get his guns fixed, a thing that many a pilot might have done with prudence and good reason, but Welch kept on with that minimum of thirty-calibre fire power, and shot down the enemy dive bomber.

His own plane was hit. An incendiary bullet just missed him, and smashed into the baggage compartment at the back of his seat. He swung upward, climbed into clouds to be safe, and checked his plane. Okay. Still not bothering to return and have his guns fixed, he plunged down through the clouds to the attack again. He spotted an enemy bomber running out to sea, chased it, shot it down into the ocean.

By now, no more Japs were left in that vicinity, and Welch felt it proper now to return to Wheeler Field; the more so since he had to refuel and get more ammunition. At the field his plane was being serviced, when a wave of fifteen bombers came speeding low to the attack. Three struck at Welch's plane on the ground. He took off under fire.

He saw an American plane in trouble, a Japanese attacking it from the rear. It was George Welch's own pal, Kenneth Taylor. A bullet grazed Taylor's arm; he couldn't get away. Welch sped to the rescue and got on the enemy's tail, pumping lead. The Japanese pumped lead in return. Three bullets ripped into Welch's fighter, hitting the motor, propeller, and cowling. It was a flaming duel of guns until the enemy plunged, shot down.

Having saved Taylor, Welch looked around for other game. The wave, attacking Wheeler Field, was gone. He flew over to the place where he had found the hunting so good the first time, and spied an enemy winging out to sea, bound for its carrier. George Welch shot that one down, too: four in all for him that day of December 7.

His pal, Kenneth Taylor, shot down two. One of these was a Japanese whom he had seen shoot down an American.

Months later Welch was decorated by President Roosevelt at the White House. For his Pearl Harbor efforts? Yes, but those were not all to his credit. He had kept on in the air war of the Pacific, and distinguished himself anew, compiling in a brief while a record of seven enemies shot down, and he was still going strong.

LIEUTENANT (j.g.) ALOYSIUS H. SCHMITT (Chaplain) U.S.N. (Deceased), Dubuque, Iowa
Navy and Marine Corps Medal

The capsized *Oklahoma*, bombed and torpedoed in the Pearl Harbor attack. Chaplain Schmitt, trapped in a compartment as the *Oklahoma* turned over, gave his life to save his companions.

OUT OF SUBLIME DEVOTION

ON THE morning of December 7 the warships lay at their moorings in Pearl Harbor, an unusual number of them. Two task forces that had been on maneuvers had come in, battleships, cruisers, and destroyers: but not the carriers. Two carriers had been delayed at sea, which was lucky for them.

The Japanese plan was to hit the defending air power first. They blasted planes on the airfields in their first surprise attack, and then had warships for targets with a minimum of air opposition. Battleships, cruisers, destroyers lay motionless as the planes of the nation with which we were supposedly at peace crisscrossed the harbor, bombing and torpedoing. American anti-aircraft batteries went into action, with magnificent courage displayed by the gunners. But such was the surprise of the treacherous assault that the Japanese bombers and torpedo planes had relatively easy targets. The great battleship *Arizona* blew up. Others were bombed and torpedoed, until they sank to the shallow bottom and lay there.

In these circumstances of ruthless havoc with little possibility of defense, there was a wealth of selfless devotion and sheer immolation. Men unable to strike at the enemy manifested their valor in deeds of fortitude and endurance: aiding their fellows, sacrificing themselves for their comrades. There was one in particular, one man whose courage was not in combat but in sacrifice.

He was ordained a Roman Catholic Priest in Rome by Cardinal Marchetti-Selvaggianni for the Archdiocese of Dubuque, Iowa. He was Curate at St. Mary's Cathedral, Cheyenne, Wyoming, and while serving there taught German and religion at St. Mary's Academy and Campion Academy. He was appointed Chaplain in the Navy with the rank of Lieutenant, and was decorated for what his citation calls "sublime devotion to his fellow men."

Lieutenant Aloysius Herman Schmitt earned his immortality at Pearl Harbor, when he was a Chaplain aboard the battleship *Oklahoma*. In the sneak punch of December 7, the old sea giant was riddled by the bombs and torpedoes and capsized in the harbor, lying over on its side.

The thirty-three-year old Chaplain Lieutenant was trapped in a compartment with other members of the crew. The water was rising, and the only way of escape was through a small porthole. Father Schmitt helped his companions out through the porthole, remaining himself until the last.

They, on the outside, were helping him through. He became wedged. They were trying to extricate him when he realized that meanwhile other men had come into the compartment. Trapped inside of the capsized *Oklahoma*, these had made their way to the compartment as their only hope of escape.

Chaplain Schmitt, wedged in the porthole, was blocking their way. He told the men outside to push him back, so that the others might get through. He insisted against their reluctance, compelled them. He dropped back into the compartment. There he urged the other trapped men on to safety, directed their escape, and gave them his blessing as they crawled out through the porthole.

They survived, but it was too late for Father Schmitt to be saved. He was caught by the rising water in the steel compartment of the capsized *Oklahoma*, and gave his life "out of sublime devotion to his fellow men."

MAJOR JAMES P. S. DEVEREUX, U.S.M.C., Chevy Chase, Maryland
Navy Cross

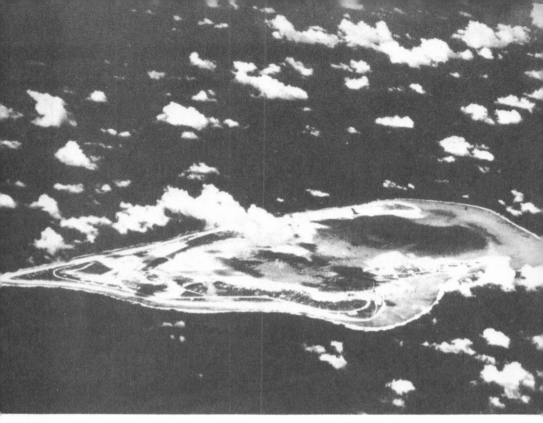

Wake Island, which 400 Marines, under Major Devereux, defended for more than three weeks against stupendous odds. They beat off repeated attacks by fleets of the sea and the sky, and at one point radioed, "Send us more Japs."

FOUR HUNDRED AGAINST AN EMPIRE

IT WAS not until the valorous defense of Wake Island had ended, that the name of the Marine commander was made known, Major James Patrick Sinnot Devereux: a rich and resounding name for a spectacular personality, international, famous Marine Corps family, birthplace, Nevada, educated in Switzerland. Major Devereux directed the battle which four hundred isolated Marines waged against overwhelming power brought to bear by the Japanese. On a remote bit of land deep in enemy oceanic territory, and with a minimum of equipment, they held out for three weeks against constant enemy assault. They fought

[15]

off seventeen separate and distinct Japanese attacks and sank four enemy warships, including a light cruiser and three destroyers. Four hundred against an empire!

On the morning of December 7 Major Devereux had just finished coffee, when the fateful message came: "Pearl Harbor attacked by Japanese. Carry out prearranged plans."

Prearranged plans! What were they? Defense to the bitter end by the tiny force of Marines, which could not possibly be relieved.

The Japanese apparently thought they would have little trouble with a handful in such a hopeless position. At noon on the day of Pearl Harbor, enemy sky squadrons came over, bombing and machine-gunning. Eight of the assaulting planes were shot down in the swirl of bombing and shooting.

That must have surprised the Japanese and given them a jarring hint of the unexpected fact that they were in for a tough time with the microscopic section of military power on Wake Island. Japan hurled warships and troop transports at Wake Island. The landing attempts were repelled with severe losses. Beating off the Japanese became such a regular thing, as the days rolled on, that at one point, when the Marines were asked if there was anything they wanted, they answered: "Sure, send us more Japs."

The fighting tactics of Devereux were exhibited best in the battle of December 11. The Japanese figured it was time to make an end to the isolated pigmy force, and set about the task in a big way. At dawn an invasion squadron of light cruisers, gunboats, destroyers, and transports appeared off the island. On shore the Marines manned their guns, and planes of the Wake Island air force took to the sky.

The invasion force moved in, shooting. Devereux had his shore guns hold their fire. Coaxing the enemy on, he permitted the assaulting ships to come in close enough to be juicy targets for shells collaborating with air bombs. Then destruction engulfed them.

The combination of shells from the shore and bombs from above sent a whole string of enemy boats to the bottom, and then what was left of the would-be invasion fleet steamed away. That was the worst day the enemy had with Devereux's absurdly small force of Marines.

It was heroic, but it could not go on forever. The Japanese could not leave the tiny band on the island, like a thorn in the side of their island realm. They had the full weight of the Japanese Empire to hurl at Devereux and his four hundred. Twenty-two days after the first attack, a powerful Japanese invasion fleet finally forced a landing, and the epic of Wake Island was closed, ending in a storm of fire and gallantry, with a huge weight of enemy numbers overwhelming a heroic few, Marines fighting until they were killed or made prisoners.

Wake Island remains a symbol for the United States fighting forces, especially the Marines: a symbol of the nation's duty of getting back at the Japanese. The enemy on that bit of seized Pacific land is a target at which American forces strike with a particular relish. Nothing pleases an American naval gunner or a warplane pilot more than to hurl blasts of high explosive against the Japanese on Wake Island.

A few weeks after the enemy seized the island, a swiftly moving task force struck a first blow of retaliation. A squadron made a dash for Wake Island, and planes took off from deck: this was in the earliest days of American aircraft carrier operation. Naval guns bombarded enemy positions, and the planes smashed them with bombs. This was one of our first successes in the sea and air war. The task force gave the Japanese on Wake Island a fine battering, and they bombed nearby Marcus Island as well.

Later on, long-distance air raids were launched against Wake Island from Midway Island, great four-motored bombers flying far to assail the enemy on the island that the Marines defended so bravely. This will go on more and more, raid after raid, and, when the eventual day of the overwhelming of Japan arrives, no success will give greater pleasure to the "Leathernecks" of the U.S.A. than the recapture of that bit of Pacific land so glorious in their history.

MAJOR PAUL A. PUTNAM, U.S.M.C., Washington, Iowa

Wake Island as it appeared to the pilots of Major Putnam's tiny air force, as they battled with Japanese aloft. This photograph was made when United States bombers struck the Japanese after they had taken the island. At the left of the island shore black smoke pours out of a bombed enemy ship.

THE FOUR-PLANE AIR FORCE

AIR POWER on Wake Island was as scarce as man power. The four hundred Marine Corps ground troops who faced all that an empire could bring against them were supported by a sky fleet of four planes—four fighters and no bombers. This quartet of sky battlers contended day after day against swarms of aerial Japanese.

At the beginning there were twelve planes which flew in shortly before Pearl Harbor. A carrier brought them to within flying distance of the island, whereupon they took off, proceeded under their own power and became the Wake Island Air

Force. Their commander was Major Paul A. Putnam, a veteran flyer of the Marines.

Ordinarily it would take many pages to name the pilots of the air force at an important point of war, but at Wake Island a brief space suffices:

Major Paul A. Putnam, Washington, Iowa
Captain Henry T. Elrod, Ashburn, Georgia
Captain Herbert C. Freuler, Orinda, California
Captain Frank C. Tharin, Atlanta, Georgia
1st Lieutenant George A. Graves, Kansas City, Mo.
2nd Lieutenant John F. Kinney, Colfax, Washington
2nd Lieutenant Carl R. Davidson, Sioux Falls, S. D.
2nd Lieutenant Frank J. Holden, Tenafly, N. J.
2nd Lieutenant David D. Kliewer, Albany, Oregon
2nd Lieutenant Henry G. Webb, Oxford, N. C.
Technical Sergeant William J. Hamilton, Altoona, Pa.
Staff Sergeant Robert O. Arthur, Burlingame, Calif.

That was the situation when the first Japanese bombing attack came on the day of Pearl Harbor. The four fighters aloft gave battle. The eight on the ground were in open temporary shelters, exposed to bombs and bullets, but nothing else was available. The swarm of enemy bombers, losing eight of their own in the assault, destroyed seven and badly damaged the other. Twenty-five men of the aviation personnel were killed. When the attack was over, the Wake Island air force, numbering a magnificent twelve planes to begin with, was reduced to four, the pigmy squadron that performed prodigies in the Wake Island sky. The Marines never had more than four planes in action: and then they had less. The day after Pearl Harbor the Japanese came out again. Major Putnam with his four fighters gave them a blazing battle, and shot down a bomber.

The high point of air action was on the fifth day of the two-week defense, the day the enemy fleet staged what was intended to be a decisive assault. Marine guns on the ground and Putnam's four fighter planes sank four ships, a cruiser, two destroyers, and a gunboat. The Wake Island air attack astonished the enemy: it was a thing to surprise anybody, in fact.

The Japanese steamed in boldly, showing no sign of fear of assault from the sky. They knew something about the killer attacks and the death-spitting guns of the Wake Island planes: their previous losses had taught them that. But they knew likewise that the Marine planes were fighters, Grummans, designed to destroy other planes, not bombers, not *hurlers* of smashing high explosive. The four-plane air force could be of no danger to warships on the water, or at least so the Japanese thought.

Putnam's fighters were transformed into bombers. The planes, in makeshift fashion, took bombs aboard, and were prepared to give the Japanese the surprise of their lives. They took off to add their own high explosive to the smashing impact of the shells of the shore guns. The enemy steamed in with serene disregard for the specks that appeared in the sky. What did the four Wake Island fighters think they were going to do? The enemy soon found out when bursts of fire and shattering concussion turned warship decks into shambles of broken bodies and twisted steel: the utterly unexpected—nothing but fighter planes, yet a bombing attack. The Japanese were completely unprepared for this, and were wide open.

The four fighters made ten bombing assaults that day. One ship they hit fled on fire, trailing smoke. Another: but that was the greatest single exploit in the epic of Wake Island. Two of Putnam's pilots, Elrod and Tharin, concentrated on an enemy cruiser. They hit it with eight one-hundred-pound bombs. The cruiser, devastated by fire and explosion, sank. This was the first large enemy vessel sent to the bottom by American naval forces in the Second World War. It was destroyed by ordinary Navy fighter planes.

That afternoon the Japanese came back again, this time with sky squadrons—not warships. Putnam's planes resumed their normal roles as fighters, and the battle was plane against plane. The aerial Marines shot down bombers, but took, as well as gave. Captains Freuler and Elrod ran into heavy fire. Armor-piercing bullets hit the motors of their planes. Freuler landed safely, and his damaged plane was repaired. Elrod crashed on the beach, his ship a total loss.

That made one plane less, but now one of the aircraft that had been damaged in the very first Japanese attack, the day of Pearl Harbor, had been repaired, and Putnam's air force still numbered four.

The day after the big naval assault Putnam's pilots drove off a bombing attack, and one destroyed a submarine. Second Lieutenant Kliewer was on evening patrol when he sighted an undersea prowler on the surface ten miles south of Wake. He took a dive at the sub, hit it with fifty calibre bullets on his way down, and as he pulled out of his dive, aimed two bombs. Both hit, and the enemy wolf of the undersea went far underwater.

On Sunday, Wake Island's seventh day, the Japanese struck with thirty-two bombers, blasted the airdrome, and got one plane, scoring a direct hit with a bomb, plane destroyed. Another of Putnam's fighters crashed on the take-off, but was repaired. The four-plane air force was reduced to three.

The next day, two giant seaplanes attacked first and then twenty-seven bombers came. The three fighters that were left shot down two; they fell into the sea. One of Putnam's planes crashed on the take-off, and was washed out. Two were left.

The next day forty-one Jap bombers struck. Late in the afternoon a four-engined seaplane dropped four bombs. It was attacked by Captain Tharin, who shot it down.

In the final attack that overwhelmed the island the two remaining fighters played their part to the end: a glorious end of bullets and unrelenting battle. One, piloted by Captain Freuler, fought to a finish with outnumbering enemy sky forces. Freuler was wounded, and made a crash landing that destroyed his plane. The other, the last of the Wake Island fighters, took off to battle, and was never seen again.

Exactly what happened to the small air force personnel left at Wake Island is not known. The culminating Japanese attack overwhelmed the garrison. The radio lapsed into silence. The airmen, like the remainder of the ground force, disappeared: an unknown number of them prisoners of the Japanese.

PART TWO

THE PHILIPPINES, BATAAN

CAPTAIN COLIN P. KELLY, JR., AIR CORPS (Deceased), Madison, Florida
Distinguished Service Cross (posthumously)
Distinguished Flying Cross

A Japanese battleship of the type that was seen in action off the coast of the Philippines when the enemy invaded. Colin Kelly spotted the hostile sea giant north of Luzon and bombed it to destruction.

COLIN KELLY

THE FIRST mightily acclaimed American hero of the war was Captain Colin Kelly, who bombed and destroyed a Japanese battleship only three days after Pearl Harbor and gave his life. His exploit excited widespread enthusiasm. Big headlines blazoned the news. The daily papers and the radios talked about it for days. The nation hailed Colin Kelly who had struck the first great air blow for America and who, in doing so, had met a hero's end.

The stories were flashed from the Philippines, and apparently the first accounts were excited rumors. They told how Colin Kelly had plunged with a swift dive into the Japanese battleship *Haruna*, and had perished in the explosion of his own bombs. This version was soon found to be inaccurate. Colin Kelly was flying a giant four-motored bomber with a crew of seven, and suicide dive bombing was most unlikely.

So what was the real story of Colin Kelly? The Army command in the Philippines made an authoritative report to Washington, a report based on an investigation that gathered all the ascertainable facts. Some angles remained in doubt, could never be known. The story, based on the official findings, was as follows:

The Japanese were making landings on the north coast of the island of Luzon, landings covered by a powerful force of warships. One of the warships was an aircraft carrier. Colin Kelly's mission was to seek out this aircraft carrier, and attack it. In his big Army bomber he flew north to the coast, and spotted transports, destroyers, cruisers, and a big battleship, but no carrier. He scouted the sea for half an hour, was not able to find the carrier, and decided to attack the battleship.

In heavy antiaircraft fire he made his bombing run, dropping three high explosive missiles. Of these one fell wide. Another hit just alongside the battleship, scoring a near miss. The third struck squarely on the deck. The sides of the battleship seemed to open, and black smoke shot upward. Masses of oil poured out onto the sea. When last seen the Japanese battleship was belching fire and smoke.

Thus Colin Kelly struck our first great air blow against the Far Eastern enemy. In the bomber there was magnificent jubilation, the crew shouting and cheering. But misfortune awaited. On its way back toward its base, the plane was attacked by Japanese fighters. The assault was overwhelming, a storm of fire. Shells riddled the bomber. The first one smashed the cockpit. Another killed the left rear gunner. Oxygen tanks in the radio compartment exploded. The empty bomb bay was set afire. Smoke poured from the bomb bay into the pilot's compartment. The heat became unbearable. The burning plane was doomed.

Colin Kelly gave the order to jump, and one after another men bailed out of the flaming bomber, taking to their parachutes. Of the crew of seven, one had been killed by enemy fire, and five reached earth safely—but not Colin Kelly. The bomber was plunging earthward, when at seven thousand feet it exploded, disintegrating in a blast of flame—with Colin Kelly apparently still in it.

Searchers found his body near the wreckage on the ground, his parachute unopened. What had happened to America's first acclaimed war hero? The official Army report states: "It is not known exactly how Captain Kelly met his death. He may have been rendered unconscious by enemy action. He may have been killed as a result of the explosion. Or he may have been struck by some part of the plane as he attempted to jump."

The acclaim that greeted Colin Kelly was the mere beginning of a long page of glory, the first of a blazing series of bombing exploits against enemy warships. We then scarcely surmised the immense wealth of valor that lay waiting in the masses of picked American youth mustered in our air forces. That first blow struck by the Flying Fortress off the north coast of Luzon occurred when we had not yet become accustomed to flashing revelations of American prowess in the air. In our first year of war any number of deeds were done that deserved applause as enthusiastic as that showered on Colin Kelly. It's good to review them, and refresh our minds with recollections of the dazzling sweep of the nation's youth across the battlefields of land and sea and sky. Or have we, perhaps, become a bit blasé from a surfeit of valor? Surely not.

SERGEANT MEYER LEVIN, AIR CORPS (Deceased), Brooklyn, New York
Silver Star with Oak Leaf Cluster
Distinguished Flying Cross

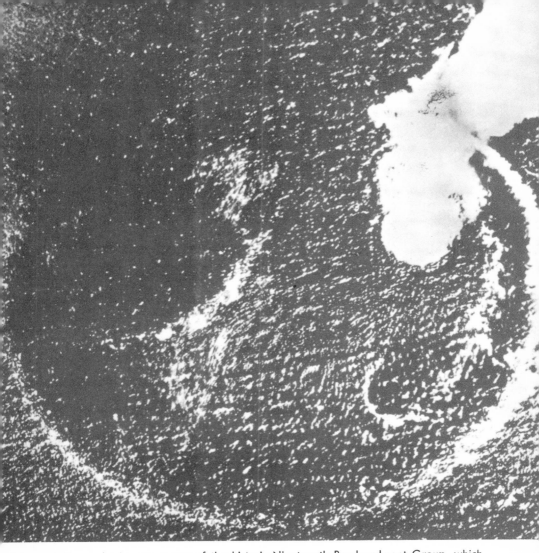

Sergeant Meyer Levin was a star of the historic Nineteenth Bombardment Group, which, time after time, pursued Japanese warships with bombs. The photograph shows how an enemy vessel tried to evade attack by circling, but was hit squarely by American high explosive.

SERGEANT MEYER LEVIN

MEYER LEVIN, called Mike, was Colin Kelly's bombardier. He it was who unloosed the bombs that devastated the Japanese battleship in the first spectacular American success of the war. He escaped from the burning, shell-riddled Flying Fortress, obeying Colin Kelly's order: "Bail out, going down." Levin told afterward how the hatch for bailing out was stuck. He found the navigator struggling with the door, unable to get it open. Together they contrived to tear the door free, at the very last moment—it was a matter of seconds, but they got out and floated to earth the parachute way.

Mike Levin carried on in the bitter sea and air fighting of the southwest Pacific. He flew and dropped his bombs in some sixty or seventy air attacks, serving in the fabulous Nineteenth Bombardment Group that bore the brunt of the early fighting in the southwest Pacific. He was in the Battle of the Coral Sea, and there had another adventure of bailing out, escaping from a Flying Fortress by parachute.

The Fortress was attacking the Japanese convoy of fifteen ships. One particular vessel was selected for a target, and the giant plane made its bombing run. Levin aimed with practiced accuracy, but nothing happened. The electrical bomb release failed to work, and nothing dropped. They tried it again, the Fortress wheeling around and coming back over the target. This time the release did not fail. The heavy bomb shot down, scored a square hit, and the bow of the big transport was blown completely away. "She was a good sized vessel," Levin said afterward, "and was easily able to carry ten thousand Japs."

All this was accomplished in the face of heavy antiaircraft fire, which Levin rated as the heaviest barrage he had ever been through. The weather, moreover, was bad. The Fortress, returning to Australia, flew blindly, and night came. Fuel ran out and finally the order was given: "All hands bail out," and out into the black darkness, and Meyer Levin made the most curious landing of all. He came down on a huge anthill, off which he scrambled in a hurry. He quickly found the navigator of the Fortress, who had floated to earth near by, and together they organized a search party and hunted for the rest of the crew, finding all of them, none injured.

The mighty bombardment group, the historic Nineteenth, lost

one man out of every three that served in it, which percentage of casualties gave a measure of its heroism. After a year of desperate bombing missions, the outfit was re-formed, and many of its veteran airmen were transferred. Some were sent home on furlough, and Sergeant Meyer Levin was on the furlough list. He never got around to taking the leave to which he had been entitled: he liked action too much. In his last letter home he wrote to his mother, Mrs. Leah Levin of Brooklyn: "I am going out again and again. Keep your fingers crossed. Pray for me."

A Fortress was going on a reconnaissance flight, and a skilled and experienced observer was needed. Levin was rated one of the keenest observers in the Pacific area. He volunteered. Not one of the regular crew, he was an extra man going along to do a special job.

The Fortress scouted a Japanese convoy, not attacking but shadowing the enemy ships, gathering that kind of precise information so vitally necessary in sea and air operations. Levin did his job, preparing a detailed report on the convoy.

The Fortress ran into frightful weather—much the same as on the previous occasion when Levin had bailed out and landed on an anthill. This time it was a case of the big bomber landing on the sea, the survivors getting out as the plane sank and taking refuge on a life raft. The other men made it, but not Sergeant Meyer Levin, who had volunteered to go along. The story of what happened as the Fortress came down on the sea, is told by the co-pilot, Lieutenant John Barbee: "I have only a hazy recollection of those last few minutes," he relates, "but I saw Levin standing, grasping the safety catches on the life raft inside the Fortress. He probably released the raft, which saved our lives, before he was knocked unconscious."

There you have the picture of Mike Levin performing his last act: releasing the life raft that saved his companions, while he himself went down with the sinking plane.

LIEUTENANT COLONEL HEWITT T. WHELESS, AIR CORPS, Fresno, California
Distinguished Service Cross

A Flying Fortress, piloted by Captain Wheless, flying over tropical coast and sea. Wheless made a single-plane attack against Japanese warships, and was ganged by Zeros. Riddled by enemy bullets, the Fortress was nevertheless brought back to an American base as a result of the almost incredible heroism of the pilot and crew.

A STORY THE PRESIDENT TOLD

ON A SMALL ranch in Texas a middle-aged couple sat by the radio and listened to a presidential fireside chat. They gave close attention to President Roosevelt's account of the progress of the war, and then came a moment when the familiar ringing accounts of the voice from the White House made them stare at each other in wonder and heart-tugging emotion. The President was relating an exploit of valor in air battle, and the hero was their son.

Among his comrade airmen Captain Hewitt T. Wheless was called *Shorty*. He was only five feet six. To his parents and the neighbors down in Texas his nickname was *Nun*. They called him *Nun* because when he was a small boy "there was scarcely none of him at all." Now the President was extolling him as a giant of courage in the air.

Captain Wheless was the pilot of a Flying Fortress that flew with four others to attack Japanese transports that were landing invasion forces on the Philippine coast, in the harbor of Legaspi. The motors of Wheless' plane developed trouble, and it lagged behind. By the time the crew got the engines fixed, the four other Fortresses had vanished on ahead. No matter, Wheless flew to Legaspi Bay. Tactics called for the big bombers to fly in formation for mutual protection, but he resolved that his lone Fortress should carry out its mission single handed.

The lone plane was ganged by Japanese. The story of what happened was told by President Roosevelt as follows: "Eighteen of them attacked our one Flying Fortress. Despite this mass attack, our plane proceeded on its mission, and dropped all of its bombs on six Japanese transports which were lined up along the docks.

"As it turned back on its homeward journey," the President continued, "a running fight between the bomber and the eighteen Japanese pursuit planes continued for seventy-five miles. Four pursuit ships attacked simultaneously at each side, and were shot down with the side guns.

"During this fight, the bomber's radio operator was killed, the engineer's right hand was shot off, and one gunner was crippled, leaving only one man available to operate both side guns. Although wounded in one hand, this gunner alternately manned both side guns, bringing down three more Japanese Zero planes.

"While this was going on," said President Roosevelt, "one engine on the bomber was shot out, one gas tank was hit, the radio was shot off, and the oxygen system was entirely destroyed. Out of eleven control cables all but four were shot away. The rear landing wheel was blown off, and the two front wheels were both shot flat."

President Roosevelt concluded by relating how Captain

Wheless brought his Fortress home: two engines gone, landing gear a wreck, the plane virtually out of contol. In addition to this the pilot had to bring the crippled giant down on a small emergency field after dark.

In Texas Mr. and Mrs. W. H. Wheless heard the story of their boy "Nun." In California two others heard it. The President concluded his eulogy of Captain Wheless with this remark—"I hope he is listening." He was. Back in the United States to visit his wife and six months' old daughter, the Captain with young Mrs. Wheless was listening to the fireside chat.

"I was floored when I heard the President talking about our ship," he said later, "but I kinda liked it though."

The tremendous fight put up by Captain Wheless' Flying Fortress might have been taken as a tip-off to the formidable defensive power that the Fortresses were to display later in many air battles. One of the surprises of the war has been the ability of those giant planes to fly without fighter support, and beat off enemy attack with the fire of their own guns. They've done it repeatedly, squadrons of Fortresses on their own, shooting their way to their targets, shooting their way out, bringing down scores of hostile planes, the Fortress formations playing their part as self-sufficient units in air battle.

This future development might have been surmised in the toughness and durability and the fire power of the big plane that was ganged by the Japanese in Philippine skies early in the war. It displayed that staunchness of construction, and that sturdy defense against bullets and shell fire which have enabled many a Fortress to get back to its base, after being battered and shot up in a way that no other type of plane could endure. Moreover, we must give credit to the staunchness of crew that figures so much in the battles waged by the Flying Fortresses.

LIEUTENANT COLONEL BOYD D. WAGNER, Air Corps (Deceased), Johnstown,
Pennsylvania
Distinguished Service Cross
Cited for gallantry

A Japanese Zero, which was forced down intact, captured by the Americans, and brought to this country for observation and study. This Zero, seen with an American pilot, is the type of enemy aircraft which Buzz Wagner shot down.

"BUZZ" WAGNER, JAP-KILLER

NOBODY KNEW HOW many Japanese planes he destroyed. He shot them down in air battles. He blasted them on the ground. Officially he was Lieutenant Colonel Boyd David Wagner, the youngest lieutenant colonel in the Army Air Force. But everybody knew the small chap with the black mustache as "Buzz." He came from Pennsylvania, and became famous as an enemy destroyer in the Philippines.

There was something coldly relentless about him, as if he burned with deep inward urge to kill Japanese and nothing else, which made him the silent avenger, the methodical killer. He spoke little about the planes he destroyed, too busy killing to talk about it, which was one reason why nobody really knows how many of the enemy he shot and blasted to oblivion. He was as if moved by a fixed idea: hunt down Japanese, bomb them, shoot them.

As an aerial tactician, Buzz Wagner was uncanny. Once two Zeros got onto his tail, and he started climbing, although he knew the Zeros could outclimb his P-40 pursuit ship. Normally it was a fatal blunder to turn upward for an escape from pursuing, fast-climbing Japanese. But Buzz zoomed straight into the sun, and the Zeros chasing him had the blinding glare in their faces. As Buzz anticipated, they climbed past him. As they swept by, he leveled off and blasted them with gunfire.

Another time three Zeros intercepted him, and blocked his way home. Buzz spotted a volcano, and that gave him an idea. He darted toward the mountain. The Japanese chased him. Buzz circled the volcano, and the Zeros kept after him. They pursued him round and round the peak. His plane was faster. He drew ahead, and presently, still circling the volcano, was pursuing them, something like a dog that is chasing its tail. Buzz was on the tail of the Zeros, and shot them up plenty.

The exploit for which Buzz Wagner won the Distinguished Service Cross was his most destructive, and it was vengeance. That time he was the killer at his fiercest, more possessed than ever with the fixed idea of hunting down Japanese, bombing them, shooting them, because he was getting even for a comrade. Two planes were on a reconnaissance mission, Buzz Wagner in one, his friend, Lieutenant Russ Church, in the other. Together they investigated an enemy airfield, diving through heavy antiaircraft fire to obtain vital information. They saw twenty-five Japanese planes on the ground, and Buzz and Russ had bombs aboard their own planes.

Two Zeros intercepted them. Buzz Wagner got one. Russ Church shot down the other, but in the exchange of gunfire Church's plane set aflame. Russ Church was doomed. He knew it, and made his end a glorious one. In his burning aircraft, he took his last dive, a fighting dive straight down at the airfield.

He dropped his bombs for shattering explosions among the enemy planes on the ground before he crashed in flames.

Buzz Wagner saw it, and later he said: "I think a man really gets mad for the first time when he sees his friends killed." Mad? It was an icy fury and lust for vengeance that drove the relentless killer in an assault of flaming destruction, a fierce urge to take lives for Russ Church's life.

Flying through a hurricane of antiaircraft fire, Buzz Wagner swept down upon the field, one single plane on a rampage of devastation. Swinging low, he dropped fragmentation bombs one after another, bombs that burst and hurled storms of shrapnel. Again and again he swept over the field, blasting planes and blowing Japanese soldiers to bits with accurately placed explosives. When his bombs were gone he raked the planes with machine-gun blasts, setting fires with incendiary bullets, and killed Japanese as they scurried about. The enemy field was blazing havoc when Buzz Wagner left it. Vengeance for Russ Church.

From the Philippines Buzz Wagner went to Australia and battled the enemy who were pushing down toward the island continent. Over New Guinea he was in one of the biggest dogfights in history, which maelstrom of air battles gave him a glowing opportunity to play his part as a pursuer and nemesis of Japanese in the hunting field of the sky. He played a star part in the engagement aloft, and shot down three enemy planes.

The gods of battle were with Buzz Wagner, but the imp of commonplace routine was not. Returning to the United States, he crashed and was killed while on a workaday flight along the Gulf Coast. The pilot, who had taken off on so many desperate missions and returned safely, left Eglin Field in a pursuit plane intending to fly to no perilous angle of war but merely to peaceful and placid Maxwell Field in nearby Alabama. He was never seen again alive. There was a long search for him, in which his father joined. Later Buzz Wagner's plane and body were found fifty miles from the point whence he started. Somehow his fighter aircraft seemed to have gone into a spin and plunged, victim of the imp of the commonplace.

SECOND LIEUTENANT ALEXANDER R. NININGER, JR., INFANTRY (Deceased), Fort Lauderdale, Florida
Congressional Medal of Honor

[40]

FAR BEYOND THE CALL OF DUTY

IN THE STORY of Nininger of the Infantry, "Beyond the Call of Duty," is the repeated theme. The young Lieutenant had no business to be in the fight to begin with. His own company was not in action. He left it and joined Company K.

It was an incident of Bataan, where, in a burst of savage fighting, weary and outnumbered Americans and Filipinos were under heavy pressure. The enemy was attacking, and Japanese snipers in trees and foxholes were concentrating a storm of bullets against Company K.

There was. bitter hand-to-hand fighting, with Company K launching an attack. Nininger, who should not have been with the company at all, crept forward and assailed parties of Japanese in foxholes, picking them off with rifle fire, blasting them with hand grenades. He wiped out the enemy in one foxhole position, and pushed on. He was wounded three times, but continued on. With a valor far beyond the call of duty, alone and unsupported, he pushed deep into the enemy position.

When his comrades drove forward and thrust back the Japanese, they found the body of Lieutenant Alexander Ramsey Nininger and around it one Japanese officer and two Japanese soldiers lay dead.

This was that same Sandy Nininger of whom his mother writes: "He was deeply religious and a boy of gentle disposition." He fought relentlessly on Bataan, fought to the death, and he it was who said before going to war: "I couldn't have hate in my heart for anyone, but I will fight our enemy out of love for my country, my home, and my church."

He was an extreme example of one type of fighting man, a soldier patriot who does his duty without fear, without hatred, without rage, a warrior who is animated by a lofty sense of dedication to the cause he believes in, the cause of his country. With that high purpose, he was in nowise content with mere duty, but went beyond its farthest call.

[41]

CAPTAIN WILLIBALD C. BIANCHI, 45th INFANTRY, PHILIPPINE SCOUTS, New Ulm,
Minnesota
Congressional Medal of Honor

A foxhole in Bataan, in which a small force of Americans and Filipinos defended themselves against a huge Japanese army. Bianchi of the Scouts was decorated for single-handed attacks against enemy positions.

BIANCHI OF THE SCOUTS

IN THE DEFENSE of Bataan, a special place of honor was won by the Philippine Scouts. They had made a reputation in previous years, and sustained it with glory against the Japanese.

The Scouts were organized by the American military authorities soon after the United States took the islands from Spain and suppressed the Philippine insurrection. Native Filipinos were recruited and trained in American army fashion. With American officers, the Philippine Scouts for years did a great job of policing the islands. They saw rough and hardy action for years. When the war with Japan came, they were a force of well-trained veterans, and on Bataan they fought like tigers.

Lieutenant Willibald C. Bianchi, of New Ulm, Minnesota, served in the Forty-fifth Infantry Regiment of Philippine Scouts. His story is another of those in which "beyond the call of duty" meant getting into a fight in which the hero had no business. In bitter battle on Bataan a rifle platoon was ordered to wipe out two strong Japanese machine-gun nests. The platoon was not of Bianchi's company. It belonged to another outfit. But he volunteered, and led one section of the rifle platoon.

In the wild, rugged country of Bataan, they pushed forward against the fire of the two machine-gun nests. Bianchi fought with a rifle. Early in the advance he wounded his left hand. That didn't halt him, although it did stop his rifle fire. With his left hand out of commission, he couldn't handle the gun. But he still had his right hand. He whipped out his pistol, firing at near-by Japs as he crept forward.

Ahead was a machine-gun nest, spraying lead. Bianchi located it, and undertook to silence it single handed—not with pistol, but with hand grenades. With a supply of grenades he made his way forward, and tossed high explosives into the Jap position. He blasted the machine-gun nest and silenced it. Doing this, he was wounded twice again. Two machine-gun bullets hit him in the chest, ripping the muscles.

He got back to his outfit, which was bringing up a tank to oppose another Jap machine-gun position. On top of the tank was an antiaircraft machine gun. Bianchi climbed on top and used the antiaircraft weapon against the strong point—firing into it. He fought the antiaircraft machine gun versus machine guns, until he was wounded again. This time enemy fire knocked him off the top of the tank, and hurled him tumbling to the ground. And then followed the hospital for Bianchi.

Some of the material about him I procured from his mother. She wrote to me and told me about the young officer who wrote his name in the hero history of Bataan. In her letter she said: "As a mother, I am proud to be able to give to this generation and to our beloved America the most precious gift that life makes possible, my only son. The son is so dear and precious to a mother," she goes on, "and for him to bring such returns to her heart, is really wonderful."

She speaks her pride and then thinks of other mothers, so many of whom have boys in the service. "I am proud," she writes, "but tell me of a mother who isn't proud of her son? They are all heroes to them. I wish all mothers could share with me the honors that have been bestowed upon me through the achievements of my son. I know there isn't any boy in the armed forces who would not conduct himself in the same courageous manner, should an opportunity present itself.

"My boy had his heart and soul in his work and dearly loved his country, the good U.S.A. My only regret," she adds, "is that I haven't four more sons to give. I have four daughters. They are all doing their bit. One of the girls is an Army nurse."

With this Mrs. Carrie Bianchi of New Ulm, Minnesota, enclosed a photograph of Bianchi of the Scouts, taken the day before he left for the Philippines.

CAPTAIN ARTHUR W. WERMUTH, Infantry, Transverse City, Michigan
Distinguished Service Cross
Silver Star
Purple Heart with 2 clasps

Captain Wermuth is here seen with his comrade in desperate adventure, the half-Filipino sergeant whom they called Jock.

The champion killer of Bataan was Captain Arthur W. Wermuth, who because of the way he brought down enemy soldiers, won the name of "The One Man Army." His specialty was getting behind the Japanese lines, and shooting and destroying.

THE ONE MAN ARMY

THE ONE MAN ARMY knew his Bataan. He came from open country, and had spent his youth in close familiarity with the primitive way of earth and sky—wandering afar over the plains and hills, the rivers and craggy uplands of the American West. He came from South Dakota, where his father owned a ranch. In the Philippines before war came, he liked to hike through the rugged country, and the wild terrain of Bataan was his favorite haunt. So, when General MacArthur drew his outnumbered men back into that peninsula, Captain Arthur W. Wermuth was ready for his role: the One Man Army.

[47]

Perhaps there was something of the American frontier tradition in the way he hunted down and killed Japs, something of the Indian fighter instinct in his daring methods of stalking Jap soldiers, ambuscading them, shooting them or closing in for desperate hand-to-hand combat. He got in among them on many a raid, a remorseless hunter of Japanese, driven by a remorseless impulse to destroy them, kill them with his own individual action. Wermuth, officer and gentleman, was a pitiless slayer, as far as Japanese were concerned.

His fame during the Bataan fighting was featured by his exploits behind the enemy lines, that being his favorite theater of action: deep in the rear of the enemy positions, where an American soldier would be the least expected and where the Jap hunting would be the best. Wermuth had a weird knack of getting through, an uncanny skill typical of the tactics of guerilla warfare, skill in passing through enemy forces, creeping and shooting his way through when necessary. He had a genius for concealment and cover, and besides, he was thoroughly familiar with the terrain, the craggy jungle land through which he had wandered so much in the time of peace.

On the sixth of January Wermuth volunteered to proceed alone to an American outpost that had been isolated by the Japanese, an American party in a desperate corner, about to be wiped out by the ruthless Far Eastern killers. This was a prime occasion for a display of the peculiar Wermuth gift. He stole through several thousand enemy troops, and found the men at the outpost which was in itself a masterpiece of getting through enemy lines. It was a mere beginning for Wermuth, who proceeded to repeat the stunt on a wholesale scale, by guiding the whole party back through the Japanese positions.

Five days later he went out on a reconnaissance patrol, and made his way behind the enemy lines. He was in a foxhole when he saw a stream of the enemy marching along a ridge near by. "I worked them over with my tommy gun," Wermuth said later, "and got at least thirty." It was a one-man ambuscade with a slaughtering of Japanese like a buffalo hunter of old, slaying the herd.

The next day, with Marine Carl Sheldon, Wermuth traveled for miles through enemy infested country, and located a hidden Japanese camp. Scouting it, he noted with satisfaction how the camp was in the range of American heavy artillery. Wermuth sent a message back to direct some shooting by the big guns, and then drew off to a safe vantage point, from which he watched a rain of shells smash the Japanese in their camp.

The One Man Army burned a town held by the Japanese. He went out before dawn with five gallons of gasoline, sneaked through Japanese positions, made his way to the town where enemy soldiers were sleeping in shacks. Moving with cool and bold deliberation, Wermuth qualified as an arsonist of war. Walking along behind the shacks, he sprinkled them with gasoline and set them afire. Then he stole away to watch the enemy habitations go up in a mass of flames.

Wermuth collected a group of kindred spirits, eighty-four volunteers, and formed a suicide antisniper unit to whom he taught his methods of stalking and killing. In accordance with their usual tactics of infiltration, several hundred Japanese had sneaked behind the American lines, and were sniping, inflicting nasty casualties. The suicide antisniper unit, using Wermuth tactics on a big scale, killed two hundred fifty of the Japanese riflemen and topped that off by destroying a number of Japanese machine-gun nests with hand grenades.

Many of Wermuth's exploits were performed in the company of Sergeant Crispin Jacob, a burly giant half Filipino whom they called *Jock*. They were an odd pair, the American captain and the half Oriental noncom, but were the closest of comrades, going on patrol together and sharing adventures of life and death peril. Jock was almost as great a stalker and killer as Wermuth himself.

It was discovered that American telephone lines had been tapped by the Japanese, a sneak party having stolen in and attached wires to the American line. Wermuth and Jock followed the enemy wire, and this led them to the group listening in. Whereupon the scene turned from telephone snooping to a savage mêlée, as Wermuth and the sergeant jumped in among the Japanese, shooting, slashing, and stabbing. In the savage combat all the Japanese were killed. Wermuth was wounded in the elbow with a bayonet, but he brought back the wire-tapping equipment.

The Japanese were making landings on the coast of Bataan, which provided Wermuth and Jock with a rare opportunity for some particularly ferocious jungle fighting. They conducted a two-man campaign against the landing parties, and that led them to what was perhaps their most desperate predicament. The two, as Wermuth later told it, "walked right into a machine gun." A bullet clipped Wermuth in the left side, went around the ribs and came out of his back. Jock was wounded too, but he never disclosed the fact. He carried the One Man Army back to the hospital, before he revealed that he himself was hurt.

On one adventure Wermuth and Jock spent three weeks behind the Japanese lines, scouting, getting information, shooting, always bringing down Japanese. All told, Wermuth was credited with killing many more than a hundred enemy troops—a One Man Army indeed.

The last seen of him was during the last days of Bataan, as the enemy were closing in. Just recovered from another wound, Wermuth had an extra pocketful of ammunition, and was headed for the fighting. He vanished in the ultimate turmoil of battle, and for some time his fate was unknown, until it was revealed later that he was a prisoner in Japan.

The military moral of the story of the One Man Army is that it takes preparation to do a job. Wermuth had readied himself for the fighting role that he was to assume. As an American officer stationed in the Philippines during the times of peace, he devoted himself to a study of what a soldier's task would be if and when the Japanese came.

His choice of the Bataan Peninsula as his favorite hiking ground was no accident. Loving the out-of-doors, he selected the terrain which he knew might be the scenes of a last stand. American strategy, with the sound idea that the enemy would come in overwhelming force, had foreseen that outnumbered Americans and Filipinos might have to retire to the proverbial last ditch, and Bataan had been selected for this. So the future One Man Army made a close study of the jungled hills and valleys of the tropical peninsula, giving himself an individual course in jungle fighting.

There is no need to fling the moral at our armed forces. They are amply aware of the value of specialized training. So are the Japanese, for that matter. They made their sweep of tropical islands largely because of the intensive jungle training they had given their troops for years, deliberately schemed preparation for wholesale international robbery. It would be good if the One Man Army could be over here to see the kind of training that our soldiers are getting. Wermuth would approve. The lesson that his story teaches is well applied in the tough and specialized schooling for war that American soldiers receive, making them ready for battle on any kind of terrain, creating an army of millions of experts who master the tricks of fighting in every kind of country, from Arctic ice to equatorial forest.

COMMANDER FRANK W. FENNO, U.S.N., Westminster, Massachusetts
   Navy Cross
   Gold Star in lieu of Second Navy Cross
   Army Distinguished Service Cross

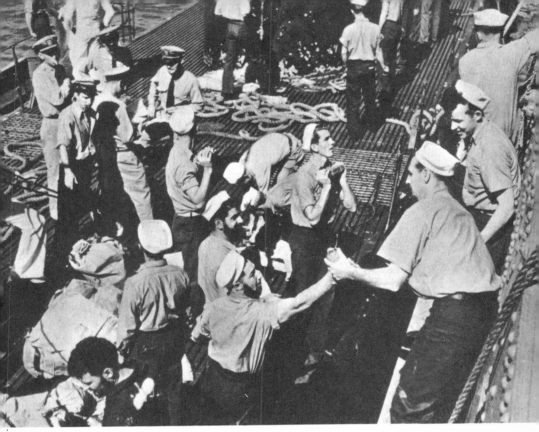

Returning to base with the Philippine treasure, the crew of the adventurous submarine takes it easy, after the eventful voyage from Corregidor to the United States base.

THE ESCAPE OF THE TREASURE

AN EPIC of war in the Philippines was the removal from Corregidor and transfer to the United States of a treasure hoard of gold, silver, and securities. The Japs were driving against the outnumbered Americans and Filipinos in the campaign made memorable by the defense of Bataan and Corregidor. They had control of the sea in those parts, and it looked as if they might capture all the wealth in the Philippines.

The Government of President Quezon had a large gold reserve, and there was an abundance of treasure in the twelve banks of Manila: loot for the Japanese, it might have seemed.

[53]

The gold reserve was in vaults at the island fortress of Corregidor. The treasure from the Manila banks was taken to Corregidor under enemy fire. How were they to get it through the Japanese blockade?

The answer was given when a steel nose poked its way into the harbor: a submarine running the enemy gauntlet. In command was Lieutenant Commander Frank Fenno, Jr. of Westminster, Massachusetts. No stripling youngster was Lieutenant Commander Frank Fenno. He was thirty-nine and a veteran of the pig boats. He had begun in the submarine service when he was twenty-seven, and had navigated in many a sea, many an undersea. Now he came to take out the Philippine treasure.

He brought something, too, a greater treasure still, in a way. His undersea craft, the *Trout*, was crammed with antiaircraft ammunition, a commodity of which the American and Philippine forces were pitifully lacking. Thanks to the *Trout*, Army batteries were able to go into blasting action, as they did shortly afterward, when their antiaircraft fire beat off wave after wave of Japanese bombers and shot down many of them.

In the dark of night at Corregidor a strange and busy sight was seen in the ghostly illumination of dim and furtive lights. Men were loading cases of gold and silver and securities into a steel hull. The task was not complete when dawn came, and it would be disastrous to disclose the spectacle to peering eyes of Japanese in planes overhead. The *Trout* put off from shore, went three miles out in Manila Bay, submerged, and lay on the bottom all through the day.

The next night a boat went out with the remainder of the treasure and met the submarine. Once again the dim scene of hasty loading was enacted, as they put the precious cargo aboard the submarine. Then the *Trout* put down its nose and went below the water.

Submerged, the undersea craft made its way through the enemy-controlled waters, running the enemy blockade, and went on across hundreds of miles of sea dominated by Japanese warships. Finally, it made a rendezvous with a cruiser, which took aboard the treasure for delivery to a United States base.

It was a fine stock of valuables which the Japanese certainly must have been chagrined not to discover—when they searched the vaults of Corregidor, and found them bare. One can imagine the fluent curses in the most profane Nipponese.

Such was the story of Frank Fenno's submarine treasure mission, but not the end of his exploits on that particular cruise. After having delivered the hoard of Philippine wealth to the United States cruiser at sea, he steered his undersea craft, the *Trout*, across the ocean spaces to waters where the danger was great, but where the hunting was good.

American submarines automatically stick their noses in the direction of those over-long sea lanes on which the Japanese must depend for transportation, the extended communication lines that are the links between Japan and the immense empire that they have seized. There the Japanese freighters ply their way in an endless succession, and there the American undersea fleet finds its happy hunting grounds, sinking ships and more ships. We realized that blows against the transport tie-up of the Japanese and his conquests are a most likely way of disorganizing the pirate empire that has been so suddenly created. That's where the enemy is mighty vulnerable. The commander of the *Trout*, adventuring in the days of Philippine warfare, was one of the first to hit the Japanese supply line.

During his cruise after delivering the Philippine treasure, Fenno had a narrow escape. He spotted a Japanese cargo ship. The *Trout* maneuvered, and fired torpedoes. In the swift bit of action, the *Trout* itself was assailed. A Japanese patrol boat happened to be near by, and came dashing to the attack. Did the *Trout* escape? Well, it didn't try to. Instead of ducking for underwater safety, Lieutenant-Commander Fenno boldly attacked the attacker. Maneuvering deftly, he got a bead on the patrol boat, and sank it with an accurate torpedo shot.

GENERAL DOUGLAS MAC ARTHUR, U.S.A.

Congressional Medal of Honor
Distinguished Service Cross with Oak Leaf Cluster
Distinguished Service Medal with Oak Leaf Cluster
Silver Star with six Oak Leaf Clusters
Purple Heart with Oak Leaf Cluster
And more than a dozen decorations awarded by different foreign countries
General Douglas MacArthur with Major General Jonathan Wainwright, to whom he
turned over the command of the American and Philippine forces on Bataan. General
Wainwright continued the defense until the inevitable end.

With General MacArthur is Philippine President Quezon, his colleague in the monumental Philippine Island fight against the Japanese.

MACARTHUR THE IDEAL SOLDIER

ON A DAY in March, 1942, a significant thing was noted in the New York Stock Market. Australian bonds took a sharp rise. For days and weeks the tide of Japanese invasion had been rolling toward the island conflict, and Australian securities had been slumping badly. But now the downward trend was reversed suddenly and Australian bonds jumped as much as forty dollars to a thousand dollars.

Why? What was the reason for the financial phenomenon? That day the news broke that General Douglas MacArthur had arrived in Australia to take command of United Nations' forces

[57]

there. The Allied world acclaimed the event with enthusiasm. Wall Street said it in the cold language of stock market quotations.

The very personality of MacArthur stimulated enthusiasm: a personality buoyant with the gifts of talent, good fortune, and success. He was lucky in the circumstance of birth, the most favorable sort of origin for an army career. His father was the youngest of the Civil War generals to stay in the Army. The father's military career was brilliant, and the son carried it on in scintillating fashion.

That he should be admitted to West Point Academy was a foregone conclusion, and at the military academy young Douglas MacArthur was a brilliant student. In the Army he more than fulfilled his West Point promise. He had a phenomenal rise in the service. In the World War he was the youngest general officer. He commanded the Forty-second Division, the Rainbow Division, and won decorations for gallantry in the thick of combat in France.

In the years that followed, his career continued its crescendo of brilliant success. MacArthur became Superintendent of West Point, the youngest superintendent the Military Academy ever had. He became Chief of Staff, achieving the pinnacle of an Army man's peace-time career. He was the youngest Chief of Staff the Army ever had.

He came to the time of retirement, and that usually writes "finis" in an officer's active life: retirement, work finished, duty done. But MacArthur was called to the Philippines to organize the Army of the Philippine Republic. He did his organization job with ample MacArthur competence, and was in a dramatic spot. War was visibly approaching in the Far East, and the Philippines would be a critical point when it came. Lieutenant-General MacArthur made a study of campaigning in the Philippines.

He was superbly qualified for the job of fighting the Japanese when they surged, an invading horde. A tough job, for everybody knew that the sprawling islands cut off from aid could hardly be defended against the power of Japan. MacArthur, assailed by a hugely outnumbering enemy, did the brilliant thing, fighting a delaying battle, and pulling his tiny army into the Bataan peninsula. Thereafter two names fired the courage of the United Nations amid their heavy reverses: Bataan and MacArthur.

There were insistent calls that MacArthur be placed in the high command. It was known, of course, that he would be reluctant to leave his little army in the Bataan Peninsula and go to Australia to take charge. But he would have to obey an order issued by his Commander in Chief, the President of the United States.

The journey from Bataan to Australia was a thriller: two thousand miles by sea and air. General MacArthur was accompanied by his wife and son, a tiny lad of four, and by several of his chief lieutenants. Mrs. MacArthur and the little boy had been sheltered at the fortress of Corregidor, that stronghold under long and heavy attack.

The MacArthur party was taken out of Bataan by the redoubtable Bulkeley, hero of the motor torpedo boats. They had a tremendous sea voyage to the southern Philippine island of Mindanao, where planes were to pick up the General and his group. Two of the small speedy boats made the trip, running through storms and towering seas, navigating by dead reckoning at night in waters studded with dangerous reefs. At one point they sighted a Japanese cruiser, but by clever work got around it.

They arrived at Mindanao for the rendezvous with planes. Things went awry. Four Flying Fortresses flying from an Australian base were to pick them up. One cracked up on the take-off. Then two were forced down on the Australian desert. One flew to Mindanao for the rendezvous, but it had motor difficulties and was compelled to go back without any of the MacArthur party. The General, his wife, and son, and the other officers had to wait for five days, every hour of the delay fraught with peril.

Finally planes arrived and took them to Australia. There MacArthur took the United Nations' command, and aroused much confidence that falling Australian bonds soared upward.

LIEUTENANT COMMANDER JOHN D. BULKELEY, U.S.N., Long Island City, New York

Congressional Medal of Honor
Navy Cross
Army Distinguished Service Cross with Oak Leaf Cluster
Army Silver Star
Philippine Distinguished Conduct Star

A Japanese heavy cruiser, a ten-thousand tonner. Bulkeley and his motor torpedo boats were death to hostile war vessels, and specialized in torpedoing cruisers.

THE INCREDIBLE BULKELEY

BULKELEY BECAME a legend in the Navy. His boldness and daring were such that sometimes they were mentioned almost with frowns. Indeed, his style of battle would have been mere rashness if it had not been for his uncanny skill and tactics. The word "expendable" applied to him and his torpedo boat squadron. Of six boats each manned by a crew of twelve, most of the men and all of the boats were expended. Bulkeley's squadron, Motor Torpedo Squadron Three, fought literally to the end, to the last boat.

Bulkeley liked to lay his boat alongside in the fashion of the antique sea fights of sailing ship days. He'd come speeding up beside a Japanese landing barge and battle it out in a gun fight, a daredevil shooting match. But always there was a touch of warrior method in Bulkeley's apparent madness.

One of his great exploits was the sinking of a Japanese cruiser that was bombing American positions on the coast of Bataan. Bold? Yes, but mark the tactics. Two boats, Bulkeley's and another, went out to do something about the pestilent shelling by naval guns. They had a plan for concerted action, but the plan went awry. The two boats stole at night through a maze of Japanese controlled islands, then separated. Each was to sweep around and later join in a coordinated night attack on the cruiser. Bulkeley never saw the other boat again. It ran onto a reef in the darkness, was lost, its crew escaping. So Bulkeley was alone.

His course was through tricky channels dominated by the enemy, channels that would have been difficult enough to navigate at night even under the most friendly circumstances. A searchlight on shore spotted the boat and blinked a challenge in dots and dashes. Bulkeley turned away from the danger point, whereupon Japanese artillery opened fire on the speeding craft. That raised the alarm all along the shores of islands, and thereafter Bulkeley had to run a gauntlet of searchlights and shooting. Dangerous? Sure, but also an advantage if you knew how to use it. Bulkeley knew. He used the searchlights and gun flashes from near-by shore points as guides for navigation. They located the shore for him, as he steered the boat through the tricky maze, picking his way by the lights the enemy obligingly provided.

The boat rounded a point of land. Open sea was ahead. Bulkeley ran a straight course, and presently lights blinked in the darkness. These were from the Japanese cruiser, which was flashing a light signal to challenge the approaching boat, the "who goes there" sort of thing in Japanese. Bulkeley responded to the challenge with an American answer: two torpedoes. The cruiser blew up.

Bulkeley's last feat at Bataan was the taking out of General

MacArthur, his family, and other officers. That adventure, so important for the cause of the United Nations, produced new Bulkeley headlines. He likewise took Philippine President Quezon to safety—on a trip from one of the Philippine Islands across Jap controlled waters.

Quezon tells how he was instructed by General Wainwright, the Bataan commander, not to go. Enemy destroyers were reported to be patrolling the water he would have to traverse, seven destroyers. The guess was that they had been sent to cut off the escape of the President of the Philippine Republic. But Quezon disregarded the official orders, when Bulkeley talked to him. The shrewd Philippine President studied his man. Later he said jokingly that he was impressed by the formidable black beard that Bulkeley had on his face. He looked like a pirate.

Quezon was further impressed when during the voyage a fearsome accident happened. The sea was stormy and a huge wave tossed the boat so violently that two torpedoes in their tubes were knocked loose. Their running mechanism was put into action. Driven by compressed air, their propellers whirled. This meant that at the time for which they were set, they would explode on contact. Any sort of blow on the nose would set them off.

Nice predicament. The expendables knew what to do: blow the torpedoes out with a charge of gun powder. Shoot them out into the water before the timing devices set them for explosions. But something went wrong with the gunpowder operation. There was a delay. Meanwhile the compressed air was hissing, the torpedoes' propellers were whirling, and the fateful seconds of time were running out.

Two of the crew leaned over the stern of the boat, hung by their hands and tried to kick the torpedoes loose. They couldn't do it, but the Philippine President later decorated them for their courage.

In the nick of time Bulkeley and his men were able to get the charges of gun powder set, and these blew the two perilous torpedoes out into the ocean.

LIEUTENANT COMMANDER ROBERT B. KELLY, U.S.N., New York, New York
Navy Cross
Army Distinguished Service Cross
Army Silver Star

Lieutenant Commander Kelly's P. T. Boat 32, the one in which he adventured as Bulkeley's second in command. The P. T. 32 fired the last torpedoes of famous Squadron 3.

THE LAST TORPEDOES OF P. T. SQUADRON THREE

KELLY WAS BULKELEY'S second in command. He played his part in taking out the MacArthur party from Bataan, commanding one of the two boats while Bulkeley commanded the other. He was with Bulkeley, likewise in the last exploit of Motor Torpedo Squadron Number Three. Kelly, in fact, fired the last torpedoes for the squadron, when he and Bulkeley sank a Japanese cruiser in a night attack off the Philippine island of Cebu.

They got mad that time, because they missed. Both Bulkeley and Kelly were off in their aim. The cruiser was a big one of the Kuma class, a tempting target. The two motor torpedo boats charged to the attack, and Bulkeley's boat, piloted by Ensign Cox, took the first shot with two torpedoes. They straddled the cruiser, ran on either side of it. Kelly, too, missed. That was what made them sore, and they took their annoyance out on the cruiser, making sure there'd be no more misses.

Bulkeley's boat swerved around, then charged to the assault again, pressing the attack relentlessly. Bulkeley himself aimed the two torpedoes, and both hit. The cruiser thought it was a nocturnal air assault. Its searchlight swung all over the place, looking for torpedo planes. Kelly's tactics for a second assault were the same as Bulkeley's. His aim was as good. His two torpedoes hit the cruiser, and the big ship sank.

By now, Japanese destroyers were charging at the speed boats, picking them out with searchlights and firing at them with every gun they could bring to bear. Shells knocked the mast off Kelly's boat and blasted its port side guns out of action. The port gunner was badly wounded in the throat. They got out of the beam of one searchlight, and then into the blinding ray of another which put them into a hail of fire, through which they squirmed. Those P.T. boats could flash a lot of speed when they had to, and Kelly got away into the blackness of night. That was dangerous, too, because the waters abounded in reefs, and they ran aground on a coral shoal.

There they were when daylight came, the boat impaled on coral. Nearby was the shore of an island, an island not controlled by the Japanese, and they figured they could get the boat over to the beach, and the crew would be safe, with their wounded. But Japanese planes appeared, as they headed toward the beach. The enemy bombed them, and the crippled boat had to dodge high explosive. Then the planes swooped low and machine-gunned them. The guns on the starboard side were hit so badly, they couldn't be used, and the torpedo man was killed. One of the crew shot down a Japanese plane, but the next diving aircraft hit him, and smashed his gun. A bullet raked the elbow of the chief machinist's mate, and the boat was sinking when it was beached. Only three of the crew were left uninjured, and they started taking the wounded men on shore.

The Japanese planes were still diving and shooting, and the port gunner who had been wounded first was hit again in his stomach, done for.

Under the hail of the machine-gun fire, Kelly landed the wounded and the dead, to give the latter a decent burial. He rounded up natives, had them get stretchers, and directed a trek across the island to a place from which the wounded could be sent by ship to a hospital at Cebu.

So P.T. Squadron Three fought to the last boat, after giving to the world of naval fighting a shining example of the formidable value of the swift motor boats that dash in and fire torpedoes. The history of the squadron provided a lesson of the deadly effectiveness of motor torpedo tactics. The small group of surface speedsters did the heaviest kind of damage. The Japanese ships they destroyed were many times their own value. They blazed a trail for new developments of speed boat tactics. The Navy not only cheered their exploits, but noted the instructive demonstration. Today we have swarms of P.T. boats for use in narrow waters. The equipment has been improved, new tactics have been developed, the Navy applying the lessons learned from Bulkeley and Squadron Three.

Out in the captured Philippines they talk, the Filipinos and the Japs too: talk about the swift roaring craft that laid their long white wakes on a tropical sea, that stole in and out of jungle shrouded channels, and launched their shattering torpedoes in the boldest of adventures.

LIEUTENANT (j.g.) ANNA BERNATITUS (Chief Nurse), U.S.N., Exeter, Pennsylvania
Legion of Merit (Fourth Degree)

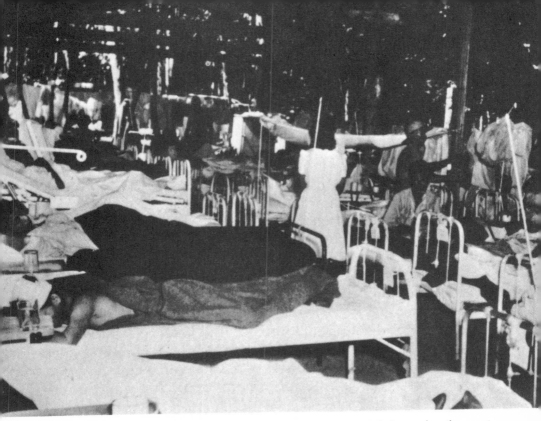

An improvised hospital in Bataan, where the wounded were cared for under the most difficult conditions in which Navy nurse Anna Bernatitus won military honors for heroic service in unremitting devotion.

HEROINE OF MERCY

THE FIRST PERSON to receive the Legion of Merit Award was a woman. That decoration was created as a successor to a military honor established by George Washington in 1782. Its purpose was to give recognition to members of the armed forces for heroic services when not in battle, not in action against the enemy. Who should better deserve that noncombat medal than a nurse: a nurse of Bataan?

Anna Bernatitus of Exeter, Pennsylvania was one of the best qualified of Navy nurses. She went through the full gamut of study as a surgical assistant, and had ample experience in Navy

[69]

hospitals. In the summer of 1940 Anna Bernatitus was sent to the Philippines to do Navy nursing there. Fate took her to the spot where the storm of war was about to break with devilish fury.

Nurse Bernatitus served from the day the Japanese attacked to the end of the defense in the Philippines. She took care of the wounded in the fighting that led to the necessary abandonment of Manila. General MacArthur led his outnumbered forces to the Bataan Peninsula for the monumental defense. Bataan was the supreme ordeal for the hospital corps, and Anna Bernatitus won her glory there.

She was number one in the small group of nurses who labored with devoted valor in the hellish fury of war. Nurse Bernatitus worked every day from dawn until midnight, caring for the American and Filipino wounded. She was no less solicitous of the enemy wounded, Japanese casualties of battle in need of medical aid. In one period of eight hours she saw two hundred eighty-five persons brought into the operating room where she assisted the surgeons.

Anna Bernatitus went through the horror and heroism of Bataan until the last few days. Shortly before the end, she was transferred to Corregidor. The island fortress continued to fight, and Anna Bernatitus continued her work of mercy.

When Corregidor fell the ace of nurses was reported missing: killed or captured by the Japanese. Then she reappeared. She had escaped from Corregidor by submarine.

Two days before the fortress fell, a few persons were selected for an attempt to run the Japanese blockade. Among those chosen was the number one nurse of Bataan and Corregidor, and she reappeared, after a submarine voyage of fourteen days through water dominated by the enemy.

PART THREE

THE WAR OF THE UNDERSEA

ENSIGN DONALD F. MASON, U.S.N., Rochester, Minnesota
Distinguished Flying Cross
Gold Star in lieu of Second Distinguished Flying Cross

A U-boat about to take its final plunge after a fight with a convoy. A Coast Guard
boat takes away the rescued German crew.

A MAN OF FEW WORDS

THE APPEAL of a phrase was illustrated vividly when in January,
after Pearl Harbor, the nation chuckled over four brief words:
"Sighted sub, sank same." That had a fine savor of informality:
it was so different from the measured dignity of a naval com-
muniqué.

Aviation Chief Machinist Mate Donald Mason was piloting a
Navy plane in the antisubmarine patrol off the Atlantic coast.
The Nazi U-boat campaign on this side of the Atlantic was in
the first phase of its destructive havoc. Donald Mason was flying
low when he spotted the periscope of an enemy undersea craft.

He dropped two depth charges, and his aim was accurate. The two giant explosions burst on each side of the periscope. The stricken U-boat staggered to the surface and then disappeared, leaving masses of oil floating on the water. The Navy listed the underwater prowler as "undoubtedly destroyed." Aviation Chief Machinist Mate Mason told the story with that breezy informality: "Sighted sub, sank same."

Little more than a month later, Donald Mason repeated his U-boat sinking performance. He caught an incautious submarine lying on the surface, flew over it, and aimed his depth charges. Clouds of smoke and spray leaped high. When the commotion died down, the wolf of the deep was seen to be a mass of wreckage lying on the surface. The Aviation Chief Machinist Mate was promoted, and continued on the antisubmarine patrol as Ensign Donald Mason.

"Sighted sub, sank same" was an early headline in the stream of news that tells of one of the major phases of the war, the battle against the submarines. Nazi Hitler has thrown the resources of war-geared Germany into a supreme effort to break the allied lifeline across the Atlantic. Any offensive against the fortress of Europe must be backed by an enormous transport of supplies, and if Hitler can stop that, Hitler is saved. Our Navy is faced with one of the gravest of naval tasks, that of keeping the convoy line open, the convoy line to Britain and to Soviet Russia.

Every sort of weapon has been pressed into service, destroyers, corvettes, patrol boats of all sorts, fleets of planes, squadrons of blimps, and that newest of aerial devices, the helicopter. Savage convoy battles are fought. The convoy moves across gray waters, across the long lines of freighters and the vigilant escort boats. An alarm, the crash of an exploding torpedo! The speedy craft on guard dash to the attack. Depth charges send huge fountains spouting out of the sea. They also send submarines to the bottom. The wolf packs are so bold, especially at night, that they surface in the midst of the convoy and fire torpedoes. Severe losses are sustained by the cargo vessels and inflicted on the U-boats.

Shipbuilding and submarine hunting are dominant features in the issue of the war. We are practicing both successfully. The men who battle against the wolf packs of the undersea have had many occasions during America's first year of war to flash the kind of news that Mason so briefly phrased: "Sighted sub, sank same." Today the Nazi U-boat campaign has been checked. The enemy attributes this to the work of the anti-submarine air patrol of which Mason is a star.

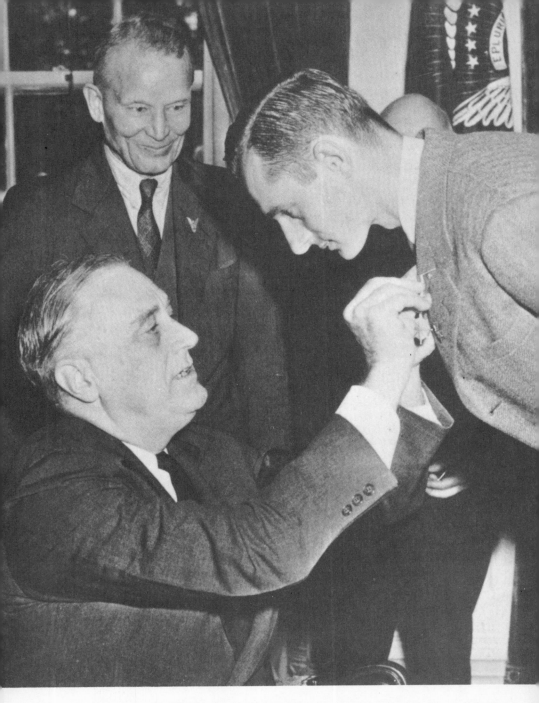

EDWIN F. CHENEY, JR., Seaman, Merchant Marine, Yeadon, Pennsylvania
Merchant Marine Distinguished Service Medal
The Medal being conferred on him by President Roosevelt in the White House

Burning oil from a tanker spurts on the sea. Into a spread of flaming oil such as this, Sailor Cheney dived to save comrades caught in the blaze. It seems almost unbelievable that anyone could survive in that inferno, but Cheney beat his way through the blazing oil.

THROUGH THE FLAMES

THE NATION TOOK action to honor the courage of sailors who man the cargo ships, the warriors in the battle of transport. Thus the Merchant Marine Distinguished Service Medal was created. The first to receive this medal was Edwin F. Cheney, Jr. of Yeadon, Pennsylvania.

Merchant mariners are heroes who have little opportunity to shoot. Rather they are targets, targets for those most devastating of missiles, the torpedoes. Theirs is the valor of endurance. Escaping from sinking, burning ships, drifting on the sea in open boats, these are ordeals that the merchant mariners face.

[77]

A big oil tanker was navigating in the Atlantic Ocean at night. A torpedo hit it amidships, and huge fountains of oil shot high. Some of the lifeboats were smashed by the explosion; others were filled with the tons of oil that geysered upward and fell in torrents. The captain issued the order: "Abandon ship." That was not so easy, however.

Ed Cheney was quartermaster of the tanker, and his boat station was aft. Flames spurted suddenly, the torpedoed tanker caught fire, and the blaze swept the deck. Cheney and all the other men were trapped.

Their only hope of escape was a life raft. Cheney launched this, but the life raft shot out and drifted two hundred feet. Soon the water was covered with burning oil, and in the twinkling of an eye the raft caught fire. There they were in a fantastic inferno of night, ocean, and flame. The raft, their only hope, was two hundred feet distant, across two hundred feet of fire, a mass of burning wood.

Cheney dived overboard, headfirst, into the blazing sea. He swam under water as long as he could, but when he rose to the surface to breathe he found himself in burning oil. Although badly scathed by the flames, he came up several times, each time, however, receiving severe burns about the head and arms. He was a powerful swimmer and displayed an uncanny sense of direction, yet it seems like a miracle that he finally made his way to the raft.

Reaching the raft, he dashed water on it with his hands, and managed to extinguish the flames. Now he was safe—or was he? Cheney did not consider himself safe until he was sure the other men were out of danger also.

Men who had been with him on the deck and had taken the plunge were his comrades in this fiery peril. A mess boy named Perona lay helpless on the water, the flames rapidly closing around him. Cheney plunged under water again to reach the mess boy. He had a burden this time, as he forced his way back to the raft, towing the mess boy, but he made it.

William Pryal, unable to swim any farther, lay exhausted in the fiery water. Once more Cheney left the raft and brought

Pryal back. Six others were able to make their own way to the raft, then they helped to guide it so that Cheney himself could climb on.

The raft began to drift but—it drifted the wrong way! A strong wind was carrying it back into the burning oil. The men thought they could row away from the fire, but found that the oarlocks were missing, so they devised a way to use human oarlocks. The sailors braced themselves in such a position that the others were able to use them as the pivots for the oars. In that way they rowed out into the calm, peaceful water beyond the blazing patch.

For ten hours they drifted before they were picked up. Cheney went to a hospital, but it was not long before he went to sea again once more on a tanker, a sister ship to the one that had been sunk in flames. This second tanker was also torpedoed, and Cheney had another narrow escape. His injuries this time consisted of a broken rib.

In the hospital and out again, and he was ready to go to sea again, once more on a tanker, a sister ship to the one that to receive the first Merchant Marine Distinguished Service Medal from President Roosevelt.

Then Cheney went to sea again.

LIEUTENANT COMMANDER FREDERICK B. WARDER, U.S.N., Grafton, West Virginia
Navy Cross

The *Seawolf*, Lieutenant Commander Warder's submarine that torpedoed Japanese ships off Java. The *Seawolf*, in daring maneuvers, stole in close to shore and blasted the enemy who was making landings. During each action, Skipper Warder, from his station at the periscope, broadcast to his crew an account of what was happening.

THE CRUISE OF THE *SEAWOLF*

THE WORST POSITION in the world for a submarine to find itself when the enemy is near is in shallow water. No fate could be worse for a sub than not being able to dive deeply enough when it is being hunted. Hence, enemy warships operating in the shallows off a coast are a perilous target for undersea attack. During the attack on Java the Japanese operated warships close to shore. This was the state of affairs when the *Seawolf* came gliding along one day.

The *Seawolf* was a "pig boat," its skipper, Lieutenant Commander Frederick B. Warder, a thirty-eight-year-old West Virginian. Peering through his periscope, Lieutenant Commander Warder spotted a big Japanese landing force: transports heavily protected by destroyers. If he were going to attempt to dispose of this landing force, he would have to dodge depth bombs and also, he would have to consider the depth of the water. He found it shallow. "Extremely shallow," said the official citation.

In the shoals off the coast of Java, the ocean currents are powerful, twisting, and treacherous. A submarine is difficult to handle accurately when it is being hauled and tugged by sweeping and swerving currents. All this the skipper of the Seawolf understood with the acute apprehension of an experienced submarine man. The hazards were grave, but hazards are but playthings to the men of the pig boats.

The Seawolf nosed in under water, moving toward the tempting targets and the bedeviling dangers. The torpedoing started and the Seawolf sank a destroyer and a big transport thus striking a heavy blow against the Japanese landing operations.

Enemy antisubmarine craft were swarming all round. Depth bombs were blasting all over the place. The Seawolf tried to "duck," but could not submerge to any depth because of shallow water. It turned and twisted along the shallow bottom, maneuvering evasively against the pull and drag of the currents. It was tough going, but Skipper Warder piloted his boat to safety.

Shortly afterward came Christmas, not the Feast of the Nativity, but Christmas Island. That is a bit of tropical land in the Dutch East Indies, south of Java, which the Japanese were in the process of taking. Again it was a case of shallow water and currents, but this time the targets were cruisers. Commander Warder braved the shoals and eddies with all the more determination. He moved in to torpedo at close range, not wanting to take a chance of missing. Because of the short range, the peril was greater, as the Seawolf ducked depth bombs in currents that eddied over a shallow bottom—maneuvering in that way to lay a torpedo into a big Japanese cruiser, getting into position to shoot, and then launching the missile.

There was one factor about that exploit to excite the especial interest of a radio man, and of radio audiences too. It developed when the *Seawolf* returned to the United States to be refitted, the stories about the combat were procured from men of the crew. They told about a broadcast aboard the *Seawolf*.

Ordinarily, the crew of a submarine, attacking under water, does not know what is happening on the surface. No one except the captain at the periscope can tell what is going on. But such was not the case with the *Seawolf*. When this pig boat, under water, attacked a hostile ship, Skipper Warder at the periscope gave a running account to his crew through the sub's loud-speaker system. A broadcast to the crew given in the way an announcer gives a blow-by-blow description of a prizefight!

The story of this unusual broadcast was revealed by Electrician's Mate John J. Sherman of Westchester, New York, who told how the *Seawolf* attacked the Japanese cruisers. He pictured Captain Warder at the periscope as he gave his orders, and then told the boys what was happening. Imagine the suspense of the crew as they listened to that broadcast!

Electrician's Mate Sherman related it as follows: "The Captain told us what was going on. He shouted: 'Up periscope, down periscope, full speed ahead. A heavy cruiser is up ahead. She is about ten thousand tons. Distance about three thousand yards. I'm going to get this baby. Are you all set below? Ease the rudder two degrees left.'

"Then the Skipper gave the torpedo order: 'Fire one, fire two. Fire three.' He was silent for a moment as he peered through the periscope, and to the men within the iron shell it was a moment of nervewracking suspense. Then the broadcast continued: 'We have hit her. The Japs are manning their guns. They're firing in our direction, trying to hit our periscope. Now they're jumping over the side. The ship is starting to go down.' There was another moment of silence and suspense, and then the broadcast voice cried out, 'She is blowing up! Everybody is in the water!' "

The *Seawolf* heavily damaged two other cruisers off Christmas Island. It is supposed that one of these sank. Certainly it was no holiday for the Japanese, but it was a feast for the *Seawolf*, which sank eight enemy vessels on that one cruise.

LIEUTENANT COMMANDER DUDLEY MORTON, U.S.N., Miami, Florida
Distinguished Service Cross

The destroyer which the *Wahoo* sank at Mushu Island, off the northern New Guinea coast. As seen through the *Wahoo's* periscope, the destroyer has been broken in two by the torpedo blast. The enemy crew may be seen on the deck of their ship just before it sank.

THE *WAHOO* MAKES A CLEAN SWEEP

THAT USEFUL HOUSEHOLD implement, the broom, is not unknown as a symbol of naval warfare. Several centuries ago, on a humiliating day for England, a Dutch admiral sailed up the Thames with a broom at the masthead of his square-rigged man-of-war, thereby saying with the symbolism of the broom that the Dutch had swept the sea clear of the English. They had, indeed, inflicted a defeat on the British fleet, and the Admiral of Holland was not without justification for his mocking, boastful gesture, leading his warships into the estuary of the Thames, with a broom at the masthead of his tall man-of-war.

[85]

Nowadays the undersea warriors of the United States submarine fleet employ the homely implement of housecleaning as a symbol. When an American submarine returns to its base with a broom lashed to the periscope, the brush end aloft as a kind of banner, it means that the sub has made a clean sweep of a group of enemy vessels, sinking all of them. That was the story, and an exciting one, when the U. S. S. *Wahoo* came home disporting a broom.

The clean sweep was accomplished while the *Wahoo* was on a mission of tricky peril: war exploration, really. The Japanese were building an advance base at Wewak on the northern coast of New Guinea. Nobody knew much about Wewak or about what the Japanese were constructing there. Even the geographical location of the place was somewhat of a mystery. Wewak Harbor had never been charted, for the north New Guinea coast thereabouts was rather vague even on the best maps. Military information about the new enemy base was needed, and the U. S. S. *Wahoo* was sent to investigate: *Wahoo* exploring Wewak. So little information was available that the only way the skipper of the *Wahoo* could locate Wewak was by referring to a twenty-five cent atlas which one of the sailors of the *Wahoo* had in his possession. He lent it to the skipper, who had the Wewak sector in the twenty-five cent atlas enlarged as a working chart for navigation.

Thereupon Lieutenant Commander Dudley W. Morton of Miami, Florida, guided his submarine along the northern coast of New Guinea, and presently arrived at the Wewak sector. His method was to sneak as closely to the shore as he dared, study the contour of the coast, and with powerful binoculars try to figure out what kind of base the Japanese had built and what the shore installations were like.

U. S. S. *Wahoo* had already distinguished itself in previous operations by sinking Japanese ships. On the conning tower of the sub three rising suns were painted: Japanese flags, indicating that three Japanese ships had been sent to the bottom, one of them a warship. This time, however, Lieutenant Commander Morton's job was not one of firing torpedoes. Observation was the task now. All well and good, but what can a United States submarine skipper do when he spots a Japanese destroyer? You may be sure Morton did the right thing. The *Wahoo* was running submerged off an island called Mushu, near Wewak. Looking through his periscope, Morton spied a destroyer anchored in the narrow bay of Mushu Island. The target was too tempting to overlook. In stole the sub and fired a torpedo. It missed.

The "tin fish" that failed to find its target gave the alarm. The Japanese on the destroyer spied the long trailing wake of white. Up anchor, and they charged to attack with depth bombs. The *Wahoo* ran around under water in the oceanic game of hide-and-seek that is played so often in war of the underseas. Skipper Morton at his periscope saw a chance for another shot, and launched a torpedo. Again he missed. As the game of life-and-death hide-and-seek went on, he scored several misses. The range was too long for accurate torpedoing, but the speeding destroyer closed the range, and at eight hundred yards Morton peered through the periscope for the finisher. The *Wahoo* let go another tin fish. This time the torpedo scored a square hit. The blast blew up the destroyer, which broke in two and sank in five minutes.

There was no clean sweep about that affair, because a sub has to wipe out a group of enemy ships, not just one, to rate a broom lashed to the periscope. The clean sweep came two days later, while the *Wahoo* was still snooping around in the Wewak area on its job of war exploration. Ships appeared on the horizon, presently revealing themselves as a convoy of four. There were a seven- and a nine-thousand ton freighter, an oil tanker, and a big troop transport that was loaded with Japanese soldiers.

What followed was like a fantasy of destruction, a carnival of ship sinking on the sun-bright waters of the tropical ocean: the *Wahoo* on a torpedo rampage. Four ships were steaming along in formation, when out of nowhere the first underwater thunderbolt hit the Japanese. A huge fountain of spray, mingled with clouds of smoke, suddenly engulfed one of the two freighters.

The ship quaked and lurched, mortally stricken and sinking. The first of the four went to the bottom, the other three followed the same downward route to the locker of the wartime Davy Jones, as the series of torpedo blows struck to the end—the end of the convoy.

The transport crowded with troops sank without survivors apparently. Hundreds of Japanese soldiers were trapped below decks and drowned like rats. Other hundreds threshed about on the ocean, only to succumb when their strength was exhausted. As a killer blow, the torpedoing of the troop ship was the major event, a wholesale snuffing out of Japanese. The submarine took a shot at the other freighter after it finished off the troopship, and hit it, damaging it, but not sinking it. The freighter could wait, thought the skipper of the *Wahoo*. Smashed and crippled, it could be "polished off" at leisure. Before attacking it again, Morton sank the tanker, the oil ship taking the plunge promptly on being torpedoed.

The inconsequential detail of giving a final push to the ship already disabled was the easiest part of it all. The freighter was listing and lurching, a mere *dead meat* target, or so it seemed. Yet it was the cripple that provided the excitement. The torpedoed Japanese freighter was still able to shoot, and shoot plenty, although the aim was poor. Shell bursts scattered wide, although one nearly clipped the *Wahoo*.

"We were inclined to laugh at the freighter's erratic firing," Morton said later, "but a shot which landed right in front of us wiped the smirk off our faces." It was a long-running fight before the *Wahoo* finally succeeded in sinking the freighter at 9.00 p. m.

Of the four ships of the convoy, all were sunk, thus constituting a clean sweep in the proper sense of the word—the broom-deserving sense of the word.

By this time the *Wahoo* had used up all its torpedoes. This made it a real disappointment when the next morning the sub sighted another convoy, six this time. They had only guns with which to assail the six ships. The *Wahoo* running on the surface chased the cargo ships, shooting at them and being shot at. It was another running fight. Suddenly, a Japanese destroyer loomed in sight, and that was most disconcerting. "When you have no torpedoes," said Morton later, "you feel naked." The speeding warship charged to the attack at a fast clip, firing all its guns. Morton's description of the action is brief and to the point: "It was another running gun battle: destroyer gunning, the *Wahoo* running."

The *Wahoo* scurried away as best she could below the surface, and narrowly escaped the depth bombs.

There were injuries aboard, and these called for some heroic work, ingenious too: surgery with the doctor providing the ingenuity and the patients the heroism. The nearest thing to a surgeon that the *Wahoo* had was Pharmacist Mate, L. J. Linhe of Wisconsin. He functioned as the submarine's Esculapius, in return for which the crew gratefully surnamed him "the Quack."

One sailor, fireman H. P. Glinsky, had sustained a bad foot injury, with two toes damaged so badly they had to be amputated. The Quack had no surgical tools for performing the operation, but was a resourceful practitioner of the healing art. He used a pair of wire-cutting pliers for the amputation, and took off the toes as if he were snipping hunks of wire. Glinsky survived, though the pain was enough to kill him.

The Quack gave treatments, likewise, to the commander of the *Wahoo*, who suffered from an affliction below the back of the skull: a sort of pain in the neck. The Quack massaged Skipper Morton's neck, gave him massages every day to relieve the tenseness of muscles.

"A form of being scared, gentlemen," the Lieutenant Commander told the newspapermen later.

The *Wahoo*, having sunk five ships on the cruise, added five Japanese flags to the three already painted on the conning tower, eight rising suns in all. But the proudest symbolism was to lash the broom to the periscope as the submarine came home to its base after that clean sweep.

LIEUTENANT COMMANDER THOMAS B. KLAKRING, U.S.N., Annapolis, Maryland
Navy Cross

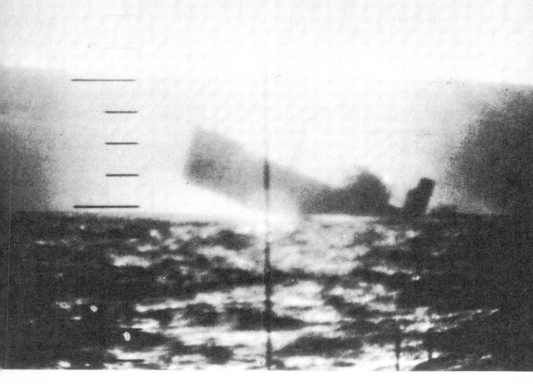

periscope view of the Japanese freighter sunk by Lieutenant Commander Klakring's submarine.

OFF THE ENEMY COAST

WHEN AMERICAN submarine men are sitting round talking, you may hear them tell how Klakring liked to take his pig boat right up against the coast of Japan. Whereupon the submarine men may continue with a discussion of horse racing. Pig boat and thoroughbred: how come? Here's the story.

Lieutenant Commander Thomas Burton Klakring of Annapolis, Maryland, took his submarine so near the coast of Japan that the boys had an idea: "We thought there would probably be racing," Klakring relates, "so we decided to take a look. Sure enough there was a big crowd of Japanese, and we made bets on the results." The betting was stretching things a little too far: it didn't work. "We were not quite close enough to shore though to see the winners," says Klakring, "but we could see the horses running all right."

After that we will not be surprised to find Klakring sinking enemy ships in the shadow of the Japanese coast. The Lieutenant Commander established records for destroying hostile tonnage.

He was cruising near land when he spotted a convoy of six iron ore vessels proceeding to harbor to deliver their cargoes to Japanese steel mills. Klakring stalked them for a hundred miles, and got in close. The thirty-seven-year-old Lieutenant Commander regards the first part of the affair as uneventful. All he did was to torpedo two of the iron-ore ships, which promptly broke up and sank.

The others scattered, and Klakring gave chase. Running on the surface, the American submarine followed two ships into a small harbor, where they took refuge, sheltered by gun fire from shore. Klakring paid no attention to the gun fire. He went right on in. One Japanese managed to get behind an island, where torpedoes couldn't get at him. The other was Klakring's mark.

The ship anchored near shore, and was a difficult target. The range was long, but Klakring didn't care if he missed. On the edge of the shore just beyond the ore ship was a power station with a great tank of illuminating gas. If the torpedo missed the ship, it would hit the power station and blow it up, and the huge gas tank would burn like an enormous torch. Lucky kind of shooting: when you miss, you hit.

Klakring's aim was precise. The torpedo crashed into the iron ore vessel amidships, and broke it in two. But now it was time to run. The American boat submerged for a fast escape from the harbor. Japanese patrol boats were swarming, dropping depth charges. There were hair-raising moments before the submarine was able to clear the harbor.

In his getaway along the coast, what should Klakring spy but another ship of the iron-ore convoy. He torpedoed and sank that one, too, getting four out of six. He boosted his total to eighty thousand tons of enemy ships sent to the bottom.

PART FOUR

AS THE JAPANESE SWEPT ON

U.S.S. Marblehead, the light cruiser that was frightfully damaged in the Java Sea. The crew, with heroic devotion, saved their ship and made an almost incredible voyage home.

THE *MARBLEHEAD*

AS THE JAPANESE swept down into the Dutch East Indies, the headline of honor went to U.S.S. *Marblehead*. That American light cruiser was in endless action during those months filled with disaster, when the enemy with bewildering speed seized a fabulous empire, an oceanic realm of incalculable wealth. The story for the United Nations was tragic, a tale of hopeless conflict against odds too great for courage to vanquish.

The Japanese were in overwhelming force, and on our side the refrain was: too little equipment, too few weapons, not enough supplies. It was a supreme example of what our men faced during the first year of the war: the desperate shortage of the means of battle, especially the utter lack of air power. The Japanese ruled the sea with powerful fleets. They mastered the sky with swarms of planes. Our men in every way exemplified the figures of speech, backs against the wall and fighting bare-handed. That's when it takes the sternest kind of valor, and they had it, as the story of the *Marblehead* will show.

A small force of American, British, and Dutch ships tried to stop the Japanese, as they steamed down to seize Java. The Allied squadrom consisted of a handful of cruisers and some destroyers. Against these the enemy were able to bring everything they pleased, up to monster battleships: their whole fleet, if necessary. It was a hopeless fight and most of the Allied warships were lost in the Battle of the Java Sea. The *Marblehead* survived only after an incredible ordeal. The Japanese claimed they sank her, stated this repeatedly, and they probably thought they had, convinced that the *Marblehead* really had gone to the bottom in the tropical ocean. Very likely the enemy believed that she could not possibly come through: few, indeed, could have believed it.

U.S.S. *Marblehead* was a light cruiser and an old one,

launched in 1923. She was lightly armored, not at all protected to withstand the violent shock of air bombing. Yet she was in a conflict distinguished by high explosives raining from the sky. A new and more violent form of the air war was being developed, and the Japanese had everything their own way at first. When the war broke, the light cruiser was in port at Borneo, and her first task was to evacuate United Nations shipping from sea areas threatened by the enemy. Then came sterner work, when the *Marblehead* joined with other Allied craft of war in trying to block the Japanese sweep upon Java.

She was in the Battle of Macassar Straits, when the squadron caught a convoy of Japanese transports crowded with troops, and sank six. That was a bad day for the enemy. Their transports jammed with soldiers were shot to pieces and sent plunging to the bottom. But the Japs had an abundance of ships and men to throw into their offensive. They took their grisly losses, sacrificing their men cold-bloodedly, and kept coming.

The Allied squadron was moving to attack a Japanese armada approaching the coast of Java, when it was assailed by a fleet of more than fifty enemy planes. The *Marblehead* took the brunt of the assault from the air. Two huge bombs smashed down on her deck, direct hits fore and aft. Another scored a near miss, which did heavy damage under water, for the old cruiser was not armored to withstand bomb explosions below the surface. The *Marblehead* was swept by fire and rocked by explosions, and water was pouring in through gaping holes in her hull. It looked as if she'd be destroyed by fire or sunk by flooding.

Then followed hours of desperate and heroic effort by the crew. They fought fire, and they pumped water. They contrived to get the flames and explosions under control, but it still looked as if the *Marblehead* would sink. Water was coming in so fast that her pumping equipment could not keep it down. The crew formed a bucket brigade and did a frenzied job of bailing for hours. This provided just the margin which kept the ship afloat while the rents in the hull were being plugged up. The steering gear of the ship was completely shattered, and they could only steer the *Marblehead* by her engines.

The cruiser contrived to limp along for three days, and reached a small Dutch port. The place had no facilities for repairing a warship. There was no possibility of putting the steering gear back into action, and the *Marblehead* still had to steer by her engines. The crew did what they could, and patched her up well enough for a staggering voyage to British Ceylon. There further repairs were made, and the *Marblehead* was able to navigate across the Indian Ocean forty-four hundred miles to South Africa. They patched her up some more, and then she continued the enormous voyage, enormous for a ship so badly smashed up. They navigated the battle-battered craft from South Africa to the United States.

She came in to an accompaniment of cheers, hailed as a hero ship. The fame of the *Marblehead* echoed from one coast to the other, the first American warship to win proud laurels in the conflict of the Pacific.

LIEUTENANT COMMANDER CORYDON M. WASSELL (MEDICAL CORPS), U.S.N.,
Little Rock, Arkansas
Navy Cross

It was through such jungle land as this that the caravan of improvised stretchers wended its way to the seacoast, inspired and led by the intrepid Doctor Wassell.

A DOCTOR'S ODYSSEY

WHEN YOU THINK of heroism in the Medical Corps, you are likely to picture a vigorous young surgeon under fire, working without halt or rest for incredible hours in a field hospital. Japanese planes are no respecters of hospitals, and he may be bombed or machine gunned as he gives medical care to the wounded.

The picture of the vigorous young surgeon does not fit Dr. Corydon M. Wassell at all. He was born in 1884; this made him fifty-eight years old when he began his adventure in the storms of battle. He had been a missionary in China, well known for his good work. President Roosevelt had described him as "a simple, modest, retiring man." When the clouds of war came on, Doctor Wassell went into active duty in the Navy Medical Corps as a Lieutenant Commander. The aging and self-effacing doctor was on duty in Java.

The Japanese stormed into the Dutch East Indies. Heavy sea fighting raged. The United States cruisers *Houston* and *Marblehead*, the latter a memorable hero ship, were in valiant action. They put their wounded ashore at Java, in charge of Doctor Wassell of the Medical Corps. He gave medical treatment to the injured sea fighters from the two cruisers, supervising their hospital care.

The Japanese invaded Java and were advancing across the island. The order came to evacuate as many of the wounded as possible to Australia. Most of them were taken out, but twelve remained, twelve men so gravely hurt that it was thought they could not be moved. They would have to remain behind, to be made prisoners by the enemy. Doctor Wassell refused to leave them. He, too, would remain behind, caring for them, and be captured by the enemy. He and his twelve patients waited for the enemy to arrive.

Some impulse of high adventure seized the doctor, the veteran missionary. His patients were in despair about becoming prisoners of the Japanese. He wondered whether they could not be taken out. The doctor thought perhaps they could: he would try. He asked each man if he would take the chance; each replied yes. Whereupon a remarkable odyssey of war was begun.

Doctor Wassell had first to get his band of wounded to the seacoast. That was fifty miles away. He improvised stretchers, and recruited natives to carry them. The country was rugged and difficult, and was under enemy air attack. The caravan of stretchers wended its way slowly for days. The sufferings of the wounded were pitiful. The doctor kept them alive with medical skill and inspired them with his courage. An official report described him in these words: "a Christlike shepherd devoted to his flock."

They reached the seacoast, where the doctor contrived to procure a small Dutch ship. He had his patients loaded aboard, and they started out on a desperate voyage. The Japanese air force was hitting at everything on the water. Planes bombed and machine gunned the little hospital ship. It seemed as if they never could get through. Japanese planes pursued them day after day.

Doctor Wassell took virtual command of the ship, and showed himself to be a navigator and a tactition. To proceed in full view on the open sea would mean sure destruction. He took his hospital ship on a course of evasion and concealment, hiding in small bays by day, and passing through inconspicuous inlets and across spaces of open water by night. He navigated the ship through a maze of tropical islands, creeping through the treacherous channels and hugging jungle-lined coasts. Thus this mild and gentle missionary, who had turned bold adventurer, got his hospital ship and his twelve wounded patients to Australia.

CAPTAIN ANDREW J. REYNOLDS, AIR CORPS, Seminole, Oklahoma
Silver Star

Curtiss P-40 is the type of ship that repeatedly matched the vaunted *Zeros*. Captain Reynolds, in his plane, shot down a series of Japanese, and grew so attached to his old bus that when it was forced down deep in the Australian bush, he wasn't satisfied until it was rescued.

SKY ADVENTURES OVER PERILOUS WATERS

CAPTAIN ANDREW JACKSON REYNOLDS admitted that he was afraid. As an Army air ace flying from an Australian base early in the war of the Pacific, he established records for shooting down Japanese as they pushed down the Dutch East Indies toward the island continent. You would hardly figure him a candidate for trembling fear. Then what made him shiver? Not the Japanese, not the Zeros and their guns. What he did not like was the water, the ocean.

The South Sea abounds in sharks, and its shores are a haunt for crocodiles. Flying over water, Andrew Jackson Reynolds often saw sharks and crocodiles, and that always gave him a shiver. He was from Oklahoma, and that was a long distance from the ocean. He was a dry-land man, and looked it: in fact, he looked like a western cowboy.

He was shot down once, but luckily landed in the bush. The air battle happened on Easter Sunday, when seven Japanese T–97 heavy bombers, escorted by six Zeros came flying from Timor, the island base north of Australia. Reynolds' squadron went after them, and started shooting down bombers. They got all of the seven big boys, not counting the Zeros, four out of the six of the babies.

Only one American pilot was lost. Another was wounded and fell into Darwin Bay, but was rescued. Reynolds was forced down, but not into any bay full of sharks and crocodiles.

His plane was considerably shot up, and came down in a buffalo wallow. Whereupon Reynolds started to walk out, through fifty miles of Australian bush. He made it, returned to his base, and immediately started talking about his plane sitting in the buffalo wallow where he had left it.

Flyers like the old buses to which they are accustomed, and Reynolds figured his could be reconditioned if the repair boys would go out and bring it back. That was one tough assignment: retrieving a disabled plane fifty miles deep in as wild a bush country as you'll find anywhere on earth. But Reynolds kept nagging. He was not happy in the new plane they gave him to fly. Finally, he pestered the repair outfit into doing the arduous salvage job. His old bus was brought back and repaired, and soon he was flying again in his familiar seat and cockpit, still leery of the water, sharks, and crocodiles.

One of the romances of the war was the abrupt shifting of homespun Americans to scenes as exotic as you will find on earth: the tropical islands southeast of Asia, the Dutch East Indies, the Coral atolls of Melanesia, the blazing wilderness of northern Australia. Youths not long out of homes in American towns and on the farms found themselves, whisked as if by a dream, into latitudes about which they had read in books of travel, onto shores that they had expected to see only in imagination: into the dank jungle with its poisonous shadow and the glint of streaming sun rays on bright tropical flowers, into mangrove swamps along the coast, into coral reefs with the flash of brightly colored fish in the shallows.

These are lands where oysters grow in the forests, where fish climb trees, where the duckbill platypus is like a beaver that has a bird's beak and lays eggs. Tossed into a world like a fantastic vision, Americans from all points between Maine and California might have thought they were on a fabulous travel adventure, save that these countries of strange scenes were desperate battlefields. Instead of sight-seeing, it was kill or be killed. Yet many a one was more ill at ease about the sinister look of the landscape, the coastal swamp, and the jungle hell, than about the Japanese and their Zeros, as was the case with sky-fighting Reynolds, who was afraid of sharks and crocodiles.

MAJOR GENERAL JAMES H. DOOLITTLE, AIR CORPS, Washington, D. C.
Congressional Medal of Honor
Distinguished Flying Cross with Oak Leaf Cluster
Medal of the National Order of Condor of the Andes (Officer) by the
　　Bolivian Government
Mackay Trophy
Harmon Trophy

The take-off from the *Hornet*, of Jimmy Doolittle, flying the first plane in the raid against Tokyo.

THE BOMBING OF TOKYO

SO IT WAS Jimmy Doolittle! I shall never forget my feeling of enthusiasm when the news came that President Roosevelt had conferred the Congressional Medal of Honor on Brigadier General James H. Doolittle, Commander of the bombing of Japan.

Our first air blow against the enemy homeland was a thing of wonder, excitement, and military secrecy. President Roosevelt's smiling statement that the American bombers had been based on *Shangri-La* dramatized the careful concealment of so many angles in the Tokyo air raid, points of secrecy to baffle the Japanese. One other thing was kept hidden: the identity of the commander of the raid. Then the secret was out, with the bestowal of the Congressional Medal on Jimmy Doolittle.

To me the marvel was that so great an assignment should have been given to so great an old-timer. Some of us had felt that, during years past, not enough recognition had been given to the veterans whose exploits had blazed the trails of flying. Save for Lindbergh, they seemed to be insufficiently rewarded, neglected. They were the daredevils of the heroic days of aviation, and none had risked his neck more often and more gaily than Jimmy Doolittle.

They called him "The Flyer's Flyer." He was the Army's ace pilot for years. He set speed records and won air races. His acrobatic stunting made many a headline. He was the first to do an outside loop, and also the first to make a blind flight by instrument alone. Jimmy Doolittle was more than a mere madcap stunter. He was a technologist who combined thrill flying with research. That's what he did in a series of experiments to determine the breaking points of planes and pilots.

"I equipped a plane with instruments to record pressures," Jimmy Doolittle told me," and put it through a series of dives and turns at high speed, the wildest kind of acrobatics. Stunting the plane, I strained it more and more, approaching the point where the wings would break. I wanted to come to the breaking point without having the wings drop right off. I ran the load up to 7.8 pounds, and when I landed, mechanics found that the wings actually had cracked, had broken: with a fraction of an inch more of pressure would have snapped off."

Risking his neck like that with actual experiment in daredevil flight, Jimmy Doolittle established mathematical formulas expressing the relation between wind pressures and breaking points of planes.

Jimmy also tested the breaking points of pilots.

"In testing the strength of planes, I also tested my own self as a pilot. How would I stand up under the same loads that would wreck a plane? In other words, how would I establish a relation between the wrecking point of the equipment and that of the pilot.

"I found that in going into a tight spiral at a speed of one hundred sixty miles an hour the pilot, with the blood leaving his brain, gradually lost consciousness, and after about ten seconds was unable to control his faculties. The first faculty to go was sight. The feeling was gradual numbness, and suddenly things got darker and darker. A few bright shooting and colorful lights were seen and finally everything became black. Today they call this the *blackout*, so common in dive bombing.

"Time and again I put the plane through maneuvers, turns and spirals, diving and pulling out suddenly, until I had gone unconscious. An instrument recorded the speed at which this occurred in different maneuvers. It was the first time that the pilot's liability to blackout unconsciousness was measured and formulas worked out."

When the Army named an old-time acrobatic flyer to organize and command the Tokyo air raid it was selecting no mere harum-scarum stunt flyer, but one of the ablest technological brains in the Air Force. Doolittle the technician directed the tremendous amount of complex organization, and devised the clever battle tactics that enabled sixteen American bombers to blast the heart of Japan, Tokyo itself, and get away from Japan without loss. Doolittle, the past master of skilful flying, led the raid, piloting the first plane.

They surprised the Japanese utterly: that was the most extraordinary feature of the Tokyo raid. The enemy had ample opportunity to detect them while they were coming in, and to mobilize the Tokyo antiaircraft defense against them, but the complete unexpectedness of the attack caught the Japanese sound asleep. Until the bombs fell, they thought the raiders were their own planes. Jimmy Doolittle tells how people on the ground paid no attention to his bomber, they just looked and some of them waved. The raiders flew at low level with ground skimming tactics of bombing. The crews could see the expressions on faces below. One plane flew over a baseball park, where a game was going on. The Japanese ball players and spectators paid no attention. American Ambassador Grew tells how he, having been taken on a mission to the Tokyo railway station, saw the Doolittle bomber skimming over the housetops. The Japanese at the railroad station looked at it and cheered: Banzai! They thought it was a Japanese army plane engaged in some particularly skilful stunt of maneuvers over the city.

Because of the bewildering surprise, there was only feeble resistance: antiaircraft fire was ineffectual, and defending Zeros, futile. The raiders, trained efficiently by Doolittle, carried out their mission with technical perfection, each plane blasting the target assigned to it, with a consequent total of enormous havoc to the enemy capital.

When the veil of secrecy was lifted and the major facts about the raid revealed, the number-one point was this: the bombing of Japan was more heroic than we thought, much more. We realized all along that it was a superb deed of valor, but the American people did not know the half of it. Military secrecy, designed to conceal the facts from the enemy, also hid the full measure of the daring of the Doolittle flyers who went winging to Tokyo.

The key element was that of timing. The plan was to take off from the carrier *Hornet* four hundred miles off the coast of Japan, to take off in the late afternoon. Jimmy Doolittle, flying first, was to have arrived over his Tokyo target just at dusk. That would have meant daylight for bombing, the last minutes of daylight; and then the cover of darkness for the rest of the flight, the getaway. Jimmy, with a heavy load of incendiaries, would light huge fires on war plants and military installations, and these would guide the planes coming in later. Bombing Tokyo at dusk would have then meant a night flight across the China Sea, arriving in China in the early morning, with daylight for landing. That was the ideal plan: darkness protecting the getaway from Japan, and then a landing on the mainland of Asia at dawn. But even so, the hazards were great, and the flyers were well aware that they were likely never to return.

But the ideal plan could not be carried out, because a Japanese patrol ship spotted the bombing expedition prematurely, spotted the *Hornet* with the other warships of the task force. It had been agreed that if the enemy should discover the squadron sooner than expected, the planes would take off immediately.

The task force, consisting of cruisers and destroyers, was a mighty valuable lot of equipment over there in Japanese waters. And the deck of the *Hornet* was covered with sixteen big Army bombers. The carrier could not release its own fighter planes for protection, and what could be more helpless than a big flat-top, its deck covered with Army bombers?

Well, they sank the Japanese patrol boat, and then the planes took off. The flyers knew what they were going into, they realized the schedule they had to follow. The timing was the most dangerous that could have been devised. They were taking off eight hundred miles from the coast, instead of four hundred miles: more distance to fly with their limited gasoline. It was in the morning, instead of the late afternoon, thus putting the bombers over Tokyo at midday, daylight flying into Japan and out. This meant a maximum likelihood of being shot down by Japanese fighters and antiaircraft guns.

How did it happen that not one plane was lost over Japan? I asked Jimmy Doolittle about that, and he replied that he could suggest only one explanation: that the Japanese antiaircraft system was completely disorganized by the surprise of the attack. They had been practicing elaborate defense against air raids, but the whole thing went haywire when the crisis came: the warning system, fighter plane mobilization, and the antiaircraft batteries were completely befuddled. Because of that, the desperate peril of bombing Tokyo at midday was minimized, and the skill of the flyers did the rest, several Jap fighter planes being shot down.

Leaving Tokyo a little after one o'clock in the afternoon, the bombers had the worst kind of schedule. They would approach the coast of China at night for landing. In fact, they did not expect to reach the coast at all. Because of the extra mileage, they figured they would run out of gas some distance from the shore. The prospect was a night landing in the China Sea with the bombers sinking and the crews taking to their rubber boats, if they could.

What actually caused them to land was a violent storm, a tail wind a lashing gale that blew them on into south China, over rugged mountain country; and in the storm at night they could never hope to find a landing field. They ran out of gas in tempest and darkness among the mountains.

Some made crash landings. But in the case of most, the crews bailed out, took to their parachutes. In the driving wind and rain at night, they landed in free China, two bombers unluckily in Jap-controlled China. One went to Soviet Siberia. Crew members in free China started walking in some of the wildest country on earth. Many were weeks in getting to Chinese headquarters. It took General Doolittle, himself, three weeks.

Now add to all this the fact that, except for Jimmy Doolittle, all the Tokyo raiders were lads just out of flying school, with a minimum of experience. They had been given, in three months, an intensive training for the raid, but they were green young-sters such as tens of thousands of others who are being turned out at our air-training bases. Their original schedule called for extreme hazards. The one they had to follow was still more dangerous by far, the most perilous timing of all.

The day we learned how great their courage was began a new era of American hate for the brutal Japanese, for that day we learned that the Far Eastern murder gang had executed some of the captured American flyers who raided Tokyo. This was announced in a statement by President Roosevelt.

Two of the bombers that assailed Japan landed on Chinese territory controlled by the enemy. Each plane carried five men; there were ten in all. Of these, five were known to have been captured by the Japanese, and three others were believed to have been. Two were missing, unaccounted for. The Japanese charged that the American planes had bombed nonmilitary ob-jectives. On this accusation they put the prisoners on trial, and sentenced them to death. Most of the sentences were commuted to imprisonment, but some of the prisoners were executed.

Pearl Harbor was an infamy, but it was an act of war. It was treachery, but it was a blow struck with military meaning. The execution of American airmen who flew in the Tokyo attack was sheer savagery, wanton, without any reason save blood lust: wanton atrocity, murder. And we can echo the words with which

President Roosevelt announced the crime: "It is with a feeling of deepest horror, which I know will be shared by all civilized people," said he, "that I have to announce the barbarous execution by the Japanese Government of some of the members of this country's armed forces who fell into Japanese hands as an incident of warfare."

Promptly our Government promised the imposition of justice on those Japanese who were responsible. The official statement read: "The American Government will hold personally and officially responsible for those deliberate crimes, all of those officers of the Japanese Government who have participated in their commitment, and will in due course bring those officers to judgment."

The Japanese accusation that the Tokyo raiders bombed nonmilitary objectives was refuted completely by the President. He stated that the flyers had instructions to attack only targets of military importance. It was known that they did not deviate from those instructions.

To this I can add some things told me by General Doolittle. He explained why his warplanes did not bomb the Imperial Palace of Hirohito. That structure was a dominating object, and the American flyers over Tokyo could see it clearly. They could have smashed it with ease. But Doolittle had given them definite orders not to do so. It might have been a blow to Japanese morale if they had blasted the palace of that absurd Son of Heaven whom they worship as divine. It might have been an effective stroke of war, but the Doolittle raiders had orders from their commander not to bomb anything but military targets. It might be argued that the Japanese Imperial Palace could be considered a military target, but Jimmy Doolittle went the limit in being scrupulous. He and his men were not going to attack anything that was not definitely military according to the rules of modern war. Jimmy Doolittle told me that many people had criticized him for being so scrupulous, overscrupulous they thought. Yet how did the Japanese repay that sort of ethics? They executed prisoners, for the very things that our flyers had been so careful to avoid.

MAJOR GENERAL CLAIRE L. CHENNAULT, AIR CORPS, Water Proof, Louisiana
Distinguished Service Medal
Chinese Military Medal, by Chinese Government
Order of the British Empire, by the British Government

[114]

A "Flying Tiger" taking off for a bombing raid against the Japanese in Burma. In the service of China, the planes of the American Volunteer Group were decorated in fear-some Orient fashion. The pilots were trained by General Chennault in highly original air battle tactics.

CHENNAULT OF THE FLYING TIGERS

THE SECRET OF the Flying Tigers was to be found in the special-ized talent and training of their commander. Claire Chennault's gift was precision flying, not merely individual precision flying. He was a master of exact acrobatics performed by a group.

Claire Chennault was an "old-timer" of aviation, whose career went back to the box-kite days of flying. He was com-missioned in the Army in the first World War days, and went into the Air Service in 1920. He was one of the great Army stunt flyers in those primeval times of aviation, an individual star in acrobatics of the air.

But the bent of Chennault's talent led him to group performance. With two other Army flyers, Hansell and Williamson, he practiced acrobatics in unison: not one plane in a dizzy stunt, but three planes doing the stunt simultaneously and close together. That was a novelty for those days, and an exciting one. Chennault, Hansell, and Williamson toured the country, performing their three-in-one daredeviltry. They became popularly known as "Three Men on a Flying Trapeze." Crowds gasped, as they dived and looped, rolled and spiraled, wing tip to wing tip, the three planes stunting as if they were tied together.

This concerted thrill flying went beyond mere show business. The Three Men on a Flying Trapeze practiced military stunting in unison, group flying in the tactics of air battle. The team did precision pursuit acrobatics in the Cleveland Air Races in 1934 and again in the following year, this time Army pilot MacDonald supplanting Williamson.

Such was the specialized talent and training of Chennault when he went to China, and joined the service of Chiang Kai-shek. China had a minimum of planes and pilots. Chennault worked to procure flying machines and flying men to aid the Chinese in their long battle against the Japanese aggressor. He contrived an arrangement whereby American pilots went to China under cover of secrecy. Army and Navy flyers enlisted in the Chinese Air Force. They formed the American Volunteer Group. Chennault trained them. He taught them the one principal thing that he had to teach: group precision acrobatics, the stunts of air battle in exact unison.

The airmen of the A.V.G. were educated and ready when the Japanese went on rampage all over southeastern Asia. Burma was the key point, and to Burma they went, battling against Japanese air power there. The results they accomplished were astounding. In battle enemy planes outnumbered them many times over. The odds against them were seemingly impossible. The number of Japanese they shot down appeared to be incredible until verified completely. They earned that picturesque oriental name, the "Flying Tigers." One of the great pages in the history of America's war against Japan was written by those Flying Tigers, who presently were taken into the United States Army Air Force to continue their exploits. The secret of it all was the accurate air battle coordination taught them by that old-time past master of group precision acrobatics, Chennault.

He was equally adept in the larger fields of military organization and international dealings; adviser on war and aviation to Generalissimo Chiang Kai-shek, prominent in the higher councils of the Chinese Nationalist Government and a coworker with China's First Lady, Madame Chiang Kai-shek. Chennault and Madam Chiang collaborated in planning for greater Chinese air strength, taking counsel in how to procure more planes, more pilots, and more bombs for fighting the Japanese, an effort that the wife of the Generalissimo was later to carry on so brilliantly in a mission to the United States.

When we entered the war it was inevitable that the trainer of the Flying Tigers should be given a high American command, and today Major General Claire L. Chennault is Commander of the Fourteenth United States Air Force in China.

He now has larger duties than the training of pilots to carry out the tactics of air battles that he developed: his old Flying Tigers are competent instructors in that specialized art. Today General Chennault has to deal with a larger problem of the war in the Far East: the air defense of China as a future base for the offensive against Japan proper. Having served as air command under Chiang Kai-shek, he is now the United States Army sky chief who deals with the Chinese war leader. They are veteran comrades.

Chennault plans for that ultimate offensive that is to strike at the heart of the Far Eastern enemy. Who would understand the aerial phase of this better than the long-time chief of the American Volunteer Group who for years has commanded campaigns against Japanese air power in China. He is intimately familiar with Chinese bases that may be used for bombing Japan. Why shouldn't he be? Either he has flown from them while they were in Chinese hands or has directed innumerable bombing raids against them. That's the old Flying Tiger experience. The master pilot who made a reputation as a pioneer in precision formation flying, and who developed the study of stunting in unison as a weapon of war, has now become a major strategist preparing for the air offensive that is to strike at Japan from the coast of China.

PART FIVE

THE *LEXINGTON'S* FIRST FIGHT

LIEUTENANT COMMANDER JOHN SMITH THACH, Fordyce, Arkansas
Navy Cross
Gold Star in lieu of Second Navy Cross
Distinguished Service Medal

A Japanese, like a sky-rocket, plunges into the sea, a sight repeatedly seen from the deck of the *Lexington*. Lieutenant Commander Thach shot down a giant enemy flying boat to begin the great old flat-top's first battle.

THE DEATH OF A SNOOPER

THACH of the *Lexington* and *Yorktown*—a title to distinguish any flyer. Lieutenant Commander John Smith Thach of Arkansas won glory in the first big battle waged by the *Lexington*, and later he starred as a *Yorktown* flyer in the Battle of Midway.

In the *Lexington* epic Thach shot down a Japanese plane that spotted the American task force. The snooper was a giant, a Kawanishi flying boat with a wing span of 132 feet. Thach was away up there when he sighted the aerial monster far below. He had a companion, another American fighter plane, Pilot Sellstrum, at the controls. The two dived to the attack.

The Japanese saw them, and ducked for cover. Towering rain clouds were in the sky, excellent cover for a fugitive aircraft. The snooper went into a cloud bank and was lost from view. Thach and Sellstrum circled the edge of the cloud. Sooner or later the enemy would come out.

It was an air-war game of hide and seek, with the two Americans lurking in the fringes of the mist, and patroling around the cloud, waiting for the Japanese to stick his nose out. He did. The monster snooper ran out for a getaway, emerging about fifteen hundred feet below Thach. It was raining there, and now came action in the downpour. Thach allowed the enemy to go so far that he would not be able to double back into the cloud again, and then dived for the kill.

The Japanese was firing with cannon, but Thach kept on. His machine guns blazed. He hit the enemy gas tank. There were spursts of flame. Thach made another attack, and again bullets streamed into the Japanese. The oversized snooper erupted fire and plunged flaming into the sea.

Thus Thach was in action at the beginning of the *Lexington's* first big fight. He was in at the climax. Japanese bombers made two attacks. In the first none of enemy planes was shattered. Then came a second, and Thach whisked to the aid of the prime hero of the clash: that incredible air fighter, O'Hare. After Butch O'Hare made an end single-handed to most of the bomber formation, Thach and companions cleaned up the rest with skilful precision. He always was a precisionist in a battle, with formation technique that he practiced and taught. He was in demand as an instructor of other pilots.

In the Battle of Midway, Lieutenant Commander John Smith Thach, flying from the *Yorktown*, was in the thick of the mighty attack that destroyed three Japanese carriers. He and his companion fighters protected assaulting American torpedo planes. Zeros intercepted the torpedo planes, and the American fighters intercepted the Zeros.

In one encounter during the wild Midway mêlée, Thach fought that kind of air battle in which two planes rush headlong at each other to see who loses nerve and swerves off first. A pilot in his squadron was in trouble, a Zero on his tail. Thach swung to the rescue, and the Zero turned on him. They went at each other in a headlong rush, both firing, each hoping to shoot the other down before the collision came. They would have run into each other, save that at the last minute the Japanese swerved off, just missing the collision. As the Zero banked, Thach got a look and saw smoke pouring out of the bottom of its fuselage, smoke and flames. An enemy shot down.

It was typical that an air-battle expert of the *Lexington* should later distinguish himself with another carrier like the *Yorktown*. Today you will find veterans of the *Lexington* distributed throughout the American carrier service, regarded as top men. The *Lex* happened to be the American flat-top that was first to get into the thickest violence of sea and air battle. She was in the area northeast of Australia when the Japanese were coming down that way, for the farthest extension of their conquests were in the southwest Pacific. So the *Lex* fliers acquired experience in large quick doses. The historic flat-top was a training ground for air heroes. In the briefest of time they became veterans of sky fighting, beginning with that baptism of fire on that day when the *Lexington* got into her first fight, assailed by bombers.

LIEUTENANT NOEL A. M. GAYLER, U.S.N., Bremerton, Washington
Navy Cross
Gold Star in lieu of Second Navy Cross
Second Gold Star in lieu of Third Navy Cross

The torpedo plane that flew to attack the *Lexington*, and was shot down. It hurtled toward the sea, trailing flaming gasoline. Lieutenant Gayler distinguished himself by shooting down Japanese planes on the day of the *Lexington's* first fight. A young Navy bluejacket snapped this dramatic photograph of a Japanese dive bomber about to plunge into the sea.

HE KNEW ABOUT GUNS

LIEUTENANT NOEL GAYLER of Bremerton, Washington, was the first in history to receive three Navy Cross awards. He distinguished himself in February, March, and May of 1942, each time earning enough glory to suffice for the lifetime of most war heroes. He was the ace of that brilliant assemblage of aces of the *Lexington*. Noel Gayler, with a record of eight Japanese shot down, was the *Lexington's* top scorer. The young son of a Navy captain was in the thick of things on that February day when the great old carrier had its first fight. His part was played when the first wave of nine bombers flew to assail the *Lex*. Eight of the nine powerful twin engine bombers were shot down by the American fighters defending this carrier, and Gayler, leading a squadron, was the outstanding individual battler in the dog fight.

His citation, in telling how he engaged the enemy bombers, uses these words: "At close range and in the face of combined machine gun and cannon fire;" close-up duels of gunnery for Gayler, but then he knew a thing or two about guns, decidedly. An Annapolis man, he had specialized in antiaircraft shooting and had served as gunnery officer aboard ship, before he turned to flying. So he was wiser than average to the ways of fire-spitting muzzles and the streams of bullets and shells. His citation speaks of "combined machine gun and cannon fire." That's what the Japanese twin engine bombers had to hurl. The American fighters had only machine guns. Gayler needed all of his gunnery science in the short-range dueling. He matched his own bullet shooting aim against the bullets and shells of the bombers with such success that he shot down two, and played a star part in destroying two others. He was the ace in smashing the first wave of bombers that assaulted the *Lexington* on the day of that historic flat-top's first battle. The ace in crushing the second attack was O'Hare.

Eighteen days later, in March, the *Lexington* made a bold dash into enemy-dominated waters, and assaulted New Guinea ports where Japanese ships were concentrated. This time Noel Gayler was not content with battling against planes. He varied that with attacks on warships. In a squadron protecting torpedo planes flying against ships, he mixed it with a seaplane fighter, and shot it down. Later, with bombs aboard his fighter, he smashed up two destroyers.

They gave him a flaming greeting, hurling a storm of anti-aircraft fire. Gayler could have been reminded of his own training as a specialist in antiaircraft gunnery. His expert knowledge of the potentialities of guns that shoot at planes could hardly have made him happier, as he went winging into the hail of bullets and shells. He hit the destroyers with fragmentation bombs, and machine gunned them, causing heavy casualties.

Less than two months later came those historic days, May 7 and 8, the Battle of the Coral Sea. That famous American victory was the first of those naval engagements that surprised the world: a naval battle in which the warships were so many miles apart that they never came within sight of one another. Fleets fought it out with planes as their striking weapons, air power reaching out and hitting ships. The accent was on aircraft carriers and their aircraft.

Noel Gayler was one of four fighters that escorted torpedo planes. American torpedoes smashed a Japanese carrier, and left it a burning wreck. The four fighters ran into a whole fleet of Zeros. Three failed to returned from an utterly unequal flight, though each apparently shot down a Japanese. Gayler bagged two, damaged two others, and returned safely.

One Japanese tried the favorite Zero trick of swift climbing, but Gayler got in a snap burst of fire as the enemy was starting his upward zoom. He shot down the other in a cloud maneuver. To evade the Zero swarm Gayler hid in a great bank of mist, lying in ambush, flying in ambush. He stuck his nose out of the cloud, and saw a Zero just below. It flew into the right position for Gayler's guns. Down in flames went the Jap.

LIEUTENANT COMMANDER EDWARD H. O'HARE, St. Louis, Missouri
Congressional Medal of Honor

Smoke rising from the water in the right of this picture marks the end of a Japanese bomber, whose pilot attempted a suicide dive onto the U. S. aircraft carrier, after his plane was disabled by U. S. Airman Lieutenant Edward H. O'Hare. Smoke in the air above the warships is from bursting antiaircraft shells.

THE TACTICS OF O'HARE

THE STORY OF O'Hare of the *Lexington* was headlined in the largest of type, though no type really was large enough. He was hailed and fêted. He was the second great American air hero to be vastly acclaimed in this war. Colin Kelly was the first, but he did not live to hear the plaudits. Lieutenant Commander Edward Henry O'Hare, nicknamed *Butch*, was more fortunate. He performed his almost incredible exploit in the third month of the war, and after a while returned home to be acclaimed as the One Man Air Force.

It was broadcast far and wide how he, single-handed and

all alone, had shot down five Japanese bombers and damaged six, thereby saving his carrier. Since that first blaze of glory, a more reasonably precise estimate can be made of the tactics and skill that O'Hare employed in what the citation calls: "One of the most daring, if not the most daring, single action in the history of combat aviation."

In the *Lexington's* first battle, Butch O'Hare played no part in the beating off of the first wave of attacking bombers. With his plane in reserve, he was on the deck when comrade flyers smashed the formation, and shot down most of the bombers. Triumphant American pilots were dispersed far and wide. Some returned to the *Lexington* to refuel. O'Hare was sent up to patrol. His plane, accompanied by another, was in the sky.

That was the situation when a second wave of Japanese bombers appeared. There were nine, with only two American fighters to oppose them. He and his companion, a lone pair of planes, flew to the attack. Then it was that O'Hare's companion found his guns were not operating. All he could do was to dive to the *Lexington* and have them put in working order. That left one fighter to oppose the nine bombers. O'Hare was all by himself, and he was short of ammunition.

It would have been difficult to have devised a more perilous situation for an aircraft carrier. The way the luck broke, the Japanese appeared to have everything their own way, and things looked bad for the *Lexington*. With only one plane to defend it, the great old carrier might have been sunk that day, save for the miracle.

On the deck the men stared into the sky, and they gaped at what they saw. The single fighter plane was shooting down bombers.

The secret of O'Hare's performance as a One Man Air Force was tactical skill. Ordinarily it is taken for granted that bombers in formation are immune to anything save simultaneous attack by a number of fighters. The bombers are grouped in such fashion that they can concentrate a devastating, converging fire on any single plane. Under simultaneous attack by many fighters, they must disperse their fire, and this permits an assault.

On the face of it, O'Hare's task seemed hopeless suicide. He performed a tactical miracle. With uncanny insight, he attacked from the angle at which the converging fire of the bombers was the weakest, and timed his assaults with a phenomenal split-second precision.

The nine bombers were flying in V-formation. He picked for his target the last plane in the right leg of the V. That was where the converging fire was the weakest. He dived at the bomber from behind to shooting distance. The Japanese had cannon; he, only machine guns. His method was to stay within shooting range of enemy fire for only the shortest possible space of seconds. He dived in, delivered a brief burst of fire for only a few seconds, and with only a few bullets, a snap burst, and he was away again. The few bullets technique was the more necessary because he was short of ammunition. It was a lightning maneuver, flicking in and away. The sharpest kind of shooting was necessary, making every bullet count. Butch O'Hare figured that at snap shooting he could outscore the Japanese, and he did.

He shot down the end bomber in the right-hand side of the V-formation, swung off, returned to the attack, and shot down the next one in line. He switched to the other leg of the V, and did the same. The bombers, never swerving in spite of their losses, kept coming on, and O'Hare kept downing them. With his tactics of snap shooting, he sent five of the Japanese plunging into the sea, and was firing into the sixth bomber when his ammunition ran out. He damaged that one. By this time other *Lexington* planes were coming to his aid, and they finished off the damaged bomber. The three Japanese that were left turned and ran. O'Hare was in action for just six minutes: that is how fast hostilities in the sky occur. He shot down five planes in six minutes—sounds incredible, doesn't it? But it's true.

The story of Butch O'Hare is a tribute to American training in gunnery. If you happen to visit any Army or Navy training base where the art of aerial sharpshooting is taught, you may be astonished by the elaborate devices employed in the inculcation of the art of taking aim. The newsreels give a glimpse, for training in gunnery provides effective spectacle for cameramen.

Americans have always liked guns, a fancy that has come down from a frontier tradition. We have never quite got over the state of mind of Daniel Boone, and that fact is something to reckon with in war. In air training they exploit the American gun instinct. This is to be observed in the schooling of marksmen for bombers and pilots who, in single seater fighter planes, do both the flying and the shooting.

One device for appealing to the American gun instinct is the employment of "skeet" shooting. Students get their first training on the range where clay pigeons are tossed by a machine and shot at. Mere sport for a start, sport with that good old-fashioned American implement, the shotgun. After a class of students has had an abundance of practice at ordinary skeet shooting, the shotgun is mounted to simulate a machine gun in a plane. A student handles it as if he were a machine gunner in action, and once again picks off clay pigeons.

That is an example of many devices that are used to develop instinctive gunnery, the kind that Butch O'Hare displayed when, with hair-trigger sharpshooting, he shot down five in six minutes.

PART SIX

THE BATTLE OF THE CORAL SEA

LIEUTENANT COMMANDER JAMES H. BRETT, JR., U.S.N., Statesboro, Georgia
Navy Cross
Gold Star in lieu of Second Navy Cross

One of the great dramatic pictures of the war, the Japanese carrier *Ryukaku* destroyed in the Battle of the Coral Sea. The flat-top is erupting smoke and flames, after attack by United States dive bombers and torpedo planes. An American torpedo plane wings its way almost into the inferno, as it banks after having discharged its tin fish.

THE BATTLE OF THE CORAL SEA

THE BATTLE OF the Coral Sea was a two-day affair, May 7 and May 8. Each day was signalized by a tremendous air blow launched from that great old flat-top, the *Lexington*. The *Lexington*, herself, came to a glorious end in the Battle of the Coral Sea, but not until she had contributed those two mighty assaults in the smashing of the Japanese fleet.

Each was an operation by dive bombers, torpedo planes, and fighters. The commander of the *Lexington* torpedo-plane squadron was Lieutenant Commander James Henry Brett of Georgia. He had already distinguished himself in air assaults the *Lexington* had staged against enemy ships in New Guinea ports. Now he played a decisive part in the Battle of the Coral Sea, leading his torpedo planes in an attack against a Japanese carrier on each of the two days.

On the first day the *Lexington* hurled seventy-six planes at the enemy fleet beyond the horizon: thirty-six dive bombers and scout bombers doing dive bombing; twenty-four torpedo planes and an escort of sixteen fighters. Their target was a great aircraft carrier, the *Ryukaku.*

Brett led his squadron of low-flying aircraft through a swarm of Zero fighters and through blasts of antiaircraft fire. American fighters protected him against the Zeros, and he helped himself with his own clever tactics. The *Ryukaku,* when he arrived, had already been hit by the dive bombers, and had fires aboard. Smoke was pouring out of the carrier and drifting down the wind. Brett used the smoke as a curtain, and led his squadron of torpedo planes down under it. They flew toward the carrier against the wind, the breeze blowing the stream of smoke above them. In that way they were hidden from Zeros above and obscured from antiaircraft guns aboard the carrier.

Brett led his squadron so close to the *Ryukaku* that hits were certain, the planes making a swift turn that got them into perfect position to launch their torpedoes, those explosive fish. What ensued was catastrophic. Twelve torpedoes ripped the starboard side of the giant ship, and smashed it into a tangle· of twisted steel. At the same time dive bombers were collaborating with the torpedo plane attack, and high explosive from above was crashing through the carrier's deck. The Jap flat-top burned, exploded, was rent apart and sank.

This was the first time that American carrier-based planes had ever gone out after live game, the first American flat-top assault against an enemy warship. It was carried out by magnificent tactical skill and with decisive success. The sinking of the *Ryukaku* by the flyers of the *Lexington* was a baptism of fire for American carriers in a sea and air battle against an enemy fleet.

On the second day in the Battle of the Coral Sea, Brett's torpedo planes once again attacked a hostile flat-top. This time something slipped in the coordination of dive bombers working in unison with the torpedo planes. The weather was bad, the enemy fleet hidden by cloud and rain. The principal section of dive bombers assigned to assult the carrier failed to find it. These planes, in fact, spotted and bombed another section of the hostile fleet. The brilliant victory on the first day had been accomplished by the simultaneous attack of many planes—there had been seventy-six in all. The large number of assailants had dispersed the enemy fire, the Japanese having had so many marks to shoot at. Now on the second day the only dive bombers to collaborate with Brett were a squadron of four, with which he kept radio contact. The work had to be done by the torpedo squadron and only four dive bombers.

A Navy citation extols Lieutenant Commander Brett's "determined leadership." That was it: the unfaltering determination with which he led his squadron into the antiaircraft fire. Eleven torpedoes were discharged, and at least five found their mark.

The Japanese shooting was concentrated on the low-flying planes dropping their fish. That left the sky fairly clear for the four dive bombers. They were almost unmolested by antiaircraft fire, and scored three heavy hits. Between the torpedoes and the bombs, the Japanese carrier behaved like an erupting volcano.

This was followed by a bit of side show. One of Brett's planes had not let go its torpedo at the carrier, so the pilot informed the squadron commander. He added that he was going to use his torpedo to attack a nearby cruiser. Brett went with him, flying in as if he, himself, were making an attack, although he had already discharged his torpedo and had nothing to shoot. Why the fake run toward the cruiser? Brett was helping his comrade by drawing some of the cruiser's antiaircraft fire. He offered himself as a mark to keep some of the bullets and shells away from his companion.

On the way back to the *Lexington*, the torpedo squadron was short of gas. In the hunt for the carrier and in battle maneuvers the planes had flown farther than their supply of motor fuel had

warranted, and now it looked as if they might be forced down
at sea. They had to conserve their gas, and they slowed down to
the most economical speed to stretch out each gallon.

The laggardly pace made them a better mark for the Zeros,
which were attacking, and they had to resort to the most careful
defensive tactics. Brett kept his planes close together, flying
in a tight formation that enabled them to concentrate gun fire
from all the planes on an assailant. Keeping low over the sea,
they were almost wing tip to wing tip.

Twelve Zeros swooped down on them. When the leading
enemy got in range, he was a target for the concerted fire of
twenty-two guns. They shot him down. The remaining eleven
Zeros pulled away, and swung around for an attack from the
other side. This time again the leading Japanese was blasted
by bullets from twenty-two guns. The ten that were left flew
away. The shooting was too good.

In the Battle of the Coral Sea the pilots of the *Lexington* put
on a show that displayed the full panorama of tactics based on
an aircraft carrier. The assault of torpedo planes was coordinated with that of dive bombers, the hurlers of the tin fish flying
low against their target, while the dive bombers swooped down
from above. The dive bombing was done by two different
groups. There were scout bombers, which had tasks of recon-
noitering as well as those of assault, and there were regular
dive bombers which confined themselves to the work with high
explosive. The coordinated torpedo and dive-bomb attack was
covered systematically by fighter planes, which knocked out
the enemy Zeros that flew to assail the torpedo planes and
bombers.

Thus, when the flyers of the *Lexington* struck at a Jap aircraft
carrier, it was a highly complicated affair with a grand pattern
of maneuver. To a casual observer it might have looked like a
haphazard whirligig in the sky, but there was a system. There
was a pattern of intricate action. Each flyer was there to per-
form with individual courage, but it was courage integrated
according to methods long worked out. Magnificent personal
exploits were performed, but they were all a part of a

general scheme of things, all in harmony with a master plan of tactics.

These complexities are typical of the involved methods of modern war at sea. The element of the air has been added to that of the sea, another dimension. Squadrons of planes have been added to the warships of the fleet, and the complications of strategy are redoubled.

LIEUTENANT COMMANDER ROBERT E. DIXON, U.S.N., Richland, Georgia
Navy Cross
Gold Star in lieu of Second Navy Cross

A fire blasted wreck, trailing oil and smoke. Bob Dixon laid the first bomb on the deck of the enemy flat-top—the first of the devastating series of high explosive hits that scored an ace American victory.

THE STREAM OF BOMBERS

BOB DIXON commanded the scout bombers of the *Lexington* in the attack on the first day of the Battle of the Coral Sea. The pilot from Georgia hit the Japanese carrier first, placed the first bomb on the deck of the *Ryukaku*. Bob Dixon and his scout bombers were at eighteen thousand feet. *Zeros* from the carrier swarmed to meet them, but they were a little late. To intercept dive bombers effectively, fighters should attack them before they start the dive down. Otherwise the fighters can hardly catch them, not to any useful purpose. This is not because the fighters are too slow, but because they are too fast. The dive bombers use flaps

[141]

to check their plunge. The streamlined fighters shoot down much faster, and pass them. They can't hang on the dive bomber's tails for any real shooting.

In the attack on the *Ryukaku*, the enemy whirled to the attack just as the American planes were going into their dive. The *Zeros* plunged after them and ran ahead of them. One would dive after an American, and soon find himself in front. A stream of planes poured down, American and Japanese, with the Zeros overrunning their targets.

Japanese pilots tried to get out of the dilemma by zooming up after passing a dive bomber, and trying to hit the next one coming down. That made the stream of planes a whirl.

The first dive bomber in the procession was Bob Dixon's. He plunged to within one thousand feet of the carrier, and had it lined up perfectly. His bomb hit square on the flight deck and wrecked it. None of the planes that still remained aboard the *Ryukaku* could now take off. Dixon's bomb hit was followed by others, as the stream of dive bombers kept pouring down. He began the job that ended with the flaming destruction of the *Ryukaku*.

Dive bombing was a Navy specialty—a thing that few people knew until it was revealed in sea and air battle. The Navy worked without publicity. The attack by the plunging plane was first brought into headlines by the Germans on land, when their dive bombers blasted the way for the blitzkrieg drives that brought about the fall of France. The world was startled by the terrifying effectiveness of that form of air power, and the Nazi Luftwaffe loomed like a monster of peculiar destructiveness.

But it was typical that dive bombing, with which the Hitler war machine swept to shattering triumphs, had really been worked out in America long before, though that had never got into headlines. The Navy had experimented with tactics of planes that hurled themselves down toward the target, and discharged their bombs when near it. It had developed the procedure to high degree, and had demonstrated the effectiveness of dive bombing. But war aviation was not in such great favor then, and the Navy practice of dive bombing was hardly noticed.

The plunging maneuver was left for the Germans to put into the headlines.

However, the dive bombers of the fleet were ready when the test came. Aboard the carriers they were prepared to put their dive bomber studies into battle practice. Thus it was that, when the first major clash of sea and air power came in the Coral Sea, the stream of bombers descended upon the Japanese flat-top, with Dixon of the *Lexington* laying the first charge of high explosive on the deck.

On the second day of the Battle of the Coral Sea, Bob Dixon distinguished himself again, this time without bombing or fighting. Leader of the scout bombers, he was doing a scouting job, and, alone in the sky, hunted for the enemy naval force to be attacked that day. In cloudy, rainy weather he found it. He dogged the Japanese ships, spotting one after another and signaled full information to the *Lexington*. Zeros went after him, and single-handed he fought and dodged, trying to avoid combat, exchanging shots when he had to, and ducking skilfully in and out of the clouds. He was like a fox hunted by the hound pack, but he stuck around getting the facts, and returned to the *Lex* with mighty little gasoline left, but with much information.

LIEUTENANT (j.g.) JOHN LEPPLA, U.S.N.R., Lima, Ohio
Navy Cross
Gold Star in lieu of Second Navy Cross

JOHN LISKA, AVIATION RADIOMAN THIRD CLASS, U.S.N., Los Angeles, California

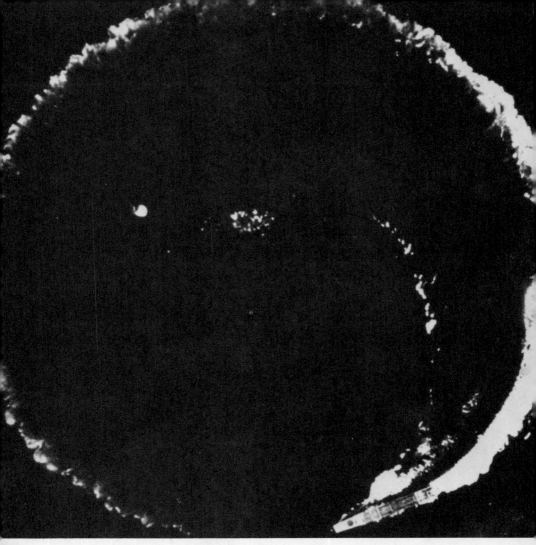

An enemy flat-top, in a desperate attempt to escape American bombing attack, makes a complete circle. Airmen Leppla and Liska did dive bombing in mass American air attacks on enemy carriers that dodged vainly in similar maneuvers.

THE DIVE BOMBER THAT BECAME A FIGHTER

DIVE BOMBERS are not supposed to be fighter planes. Their job is to take the dizzy plunge and aim their high explosive, and not to roam around shooting down enemies. Two airmen of the *Lexington*, Pilot John Leppla and Gunner John Liska, never heard about this apparently. Not content with dive bombing enemy ships, they went after *Zeros* as if they were in a P-40.

On the first day of the Coral Sea battle they were among the planes that streamed down and destroyed the carrier *Ryukaku*. Their high explosive scored a near miss. Pulling out of the dive and climbing fast, they spotted a Japanese cruiser escorting the carrier, and thought they would give that fellow a blast. Their bombing dive was one of the most eventful on record, going into a hail of antiaircraft fire, and *Zeros* were after them. Japanese fighters followed them into the dive and were on their tail, as they leveled off and aimed a bomb at the cruiser. They never saw whether they hit or missed. No time to look: the *Zeros* kept them too busy.

"There were two *Zeros* on our tail," relates Gunner Liska, "and every time they came in I gave them a blast. My gun jammed momentarily, and when it was fixed I found only one *Zero* behind us. Lieutenant Leppla saw the other *Zero* crash in the water. So I suppose I got it."

A Japanese crossed in front of the dive bomber, and Pilot Leppla shot him down with a burst of fire. Then Gunner Liska put some bullets into another *Zero*, which vanished from the fray. That made three enemy fighters shot down by the dive bomber: good going for an aircraft not meant to be primarily a destroyer of planes. But it was only the beginning.

On the second day of the Battle of the Coral Sea, Leppla and Liska again took off from the *Lexington*. This time their dive bomber abandoned its proper profession altogether, and operated entirely as a fighter. The American flat-top, having wrecked a Japanese carrier, was now being assailed. *Zeros* were swarming to the attack, and every American plane was needed to repel them.

The Navy citation describes their battle in these words: "Repeated and fierce assaults against enemy attacking planes."

They shot down three *Zeros*, bringing the total up to seven for the dive bomber that thought it was a fighter: and it was.

LIEUTENANT COMMANDER WELDON LEE HAMILTON, U.S.N., San Diego, California
Navy Cross
Gold Star in lieu of Second Navy Cross

The end of the *Lexington*—the culminating explosion, probably from a blow-up of the ship's gasoline system. Shortly before the end of the historic flat-top, Lieutenant Commander Hamilton was seen giving his bomber crews a calm lecture on the lessons they had learned in the battle.

JUNGLE FLIGHT AND CORAL SEA

THE PERILS of South Sea jungles have become commonplace—after scores of our flyers forced down in wild places have adventured in the equatorial thicket. But at first it was a fearsome prospect, with all the terrors of the unknown.

One of the first across-jungle flights occurred when the *Lexington* struck a sky blow against the Japanese in New Guinea at Lae and Salamaua. The great old flat-top pushed toward the southern coast of the long narrow island. The Japanese bases were on the northern coast. The planes flew across New Guinea, over towering mountains and dark miasmal jungles. New Guinea, so long notorious as the dark and barbarous isle, where equatorial nature at its most ferocious was exceeded in ferocity only by the man-killing tribes of Papuan cannibals.

This evil legend was amply known to Lieutenant Commander Weldon Lee Hamilton, who commanded the dive bombers of the *Lexington*. He, as it happened, had read up on New Guinea. He had gone through a stack of books telling of its jungle nightmare and cannibal horror, so he had plenty of material for imagination, as he led his dive bombers across the mountains and the haunted green of valleys. He thought of what he had read about abysmal barbarians down there, and the notion of a possible forced landing caused a shudder. Far below were thatched-top villages in the forest. Books on New Guinea told of man-eating festivals in just such places.

After such misgivings it was a relief to encounter nothing more than the Japanese enemy. The American bombers turned the harbors of Lae and Salamaua into fantasies of havoc and wreckage. Hamilton himself made a mistake, as he tells. He led his dive bombers down against a heavy cruiser, but forgot to allow for the drift of the wind. His bomb missed, a near miss. But the dive bomber coming down right behind him made a correction for the error, something like an artilleryman correcting the range. His bomb smashed on the cruiser's deck, and blew up the stern of the warship.

A few weeks later came the Battle of the Coral Sea. On the first day of the historic engagement, Hamilton, as commander of the dive bombers of the *Lexington*, led his planes against the flat-top *Ryukaku*. They were the second wave in the triumphant assault against the enemy carrier. Scout bombers had gone first, and had planted their charges of high explosive on the spacious deck, this while the torpedo planes were hurling their tin fish against the sides of the Japanese sea giant. The *Ryukaku* had been heavily hit when Hamilton and his wave of dive bombers arrived, and it was their task to finish off one of the proudest ships of the Mikado's Navy.

He led the way down, his companions following. Zeros swarmed against them, and the antiaircraft fire was a tempest.

They pressed their attack according to the relentless fashion of *Lexington* flyers, making the high-dive plunge in spite of streams of machine gun fire from the *Zeros* and in defiance of the puffs of antiaircraft shells that filled the sky.

Hamilton was a sharpshooter with a bomb, and laid his charge of high explosive in the middle of the flight deck of the *Ryukaku*. As he leveled off and zoomed upward, another of the dive bombers was in bombing position, and another ponderous mass of high explosive went streaking down to blast the enemy flat-top. Repeat that over and over again as the stream of dive bombers came down, and you have the end of the *Ryukaku*. Hamilton's dive bombers finished off one of the most formidable ships of the Japanese Navy: the first aircraft carrier to be sunk by the Americans.

On the second day of the Coral Sea, when the *Lexington*, ravaged by bombs and torpedoes, was near its end, Lieutenant Commander Hamilton gathered the crews of his squadron, and gave them a talk. He outlined tactical lessons to be learned from their experience in the engagement. It was like classroom work, as fires raged and internal explosions shook the mighty flat-top.

LIEUTENANT COMMANDER JAMES H. FLATLEY, JR., U.S.N., Green Bay, Wisconsin
Navy Cross

Seven Japanese planes were shot down, in one wild swirl of air battle. An enemy squadron of nine was sighted by four American planes. Disregarding the odds, the Americans swung to the attack. Out of the nine, they shot down seven, and Lieutenant Commander Flatley got three. The remains of a Japanese four-motored bomber of the Kawanishi type burns fiercely on the water after it was shot down in battle.

FIRST AND LAST

ON THE first day of the Battle of the Coral Sea Lieutenant Commander James Henry Flatley was both first and last for the *Lexington*. He started things at dawn by shooting down an enemy scout. At sunset he was the star of a dog fight that ended the memorable day.

Two hostile fleets, ours and theirs, were moving toward each other and were still many miles apart, but aerial eyes can see far. For the *Lexington* the first sign of the enemy was a Japanese snooper, sighted by Jimmy Flatley of Green Bay, Wisconsin, who was out scouting on dawn patrol. He reported to his carrier that he had sighted a *Kawanishi* flying boat, the usual type of long-range Japanese observation plane. The normal routine should have been for the *Lex* to send out some fighters to get the snooper. But not according to Jimmy Flatley. Taking things into his own hands, he shot down the huge *Kawanishi* on his own. It fell like a giant ball of fire, narrowly missing another of the *Lexington's* planes, which was below it.

That was how Flatley started things on the first day of the Battle of the Coral Sea. He ended it with a headline performance.

Aboard the *Lex* mess time was near. Flyers who had played their part in the air triumphs of the day were ready for dinner and a much needed night of sleep. There was talk and laughter, a comparing of notes, a careless recital of thrillers, a telling of funny ones. In the sky above the flat-top four American fighters were on patrol, keeping a wary watch for possible late-coming enemies. In one plane was Flatley, rounding out his work for the day. Clouds hung low, and it was raining. Suddenly in the murky weather the four patrol planes spied nine Zeros. Four against nine, but they swung to the attack.

The battle was fought at low altitude in the rain, from five thousand feet on down, the darting planes skimming the ocean in the downpour. One American was lost. Lieutenant Baker had been in battle in the morning, and had shot down two Zeros and a sea plane. In the murky rainy twilight he bagged another Zero, and then apparently collided with one. It seemed that he and the Zero smashed into each other. Both fell into the sea. Of the nine Zeros attacked by the four *Lexington* fighters, seven were shot down. Paul Ramsey got two. Jimmy Flatley got three, shooting them down in a swift series of sky fight maneuvers, the number one performance in the battle in the rain.

Then, as darkness closed down, the planes of the patrol skimmed back onto the deck for the night. The flyers certainly needed sleep that night. They had had a heavy day of battle, and figured it would be resumed in the morning, as indeed it was to be: the second day of the Battle of the Coral Sea. The intense strain on the airmen in such an engagement is hardly to be imagined.

On duty from long before dawn until long after dusk, getting hardly any sleep, ordered out into the sky, in air action for hours, then back to refuel and off for sky battle again. It was nerve-wracking business, but the men stood up under it, and their sheer physical endurance as well as their courage were responsible for the writing of the page of glory.

LIEUTENANT ELBERT SCOTT MCCUSKEY, U.S.N.R., Stuttgart, Arkansas
Navy Cross
Gold Star in lieu of Second Navy Cross
Distinguished Flying Cross

The death plunge of a Jap—into the water and down to the bottom. In the battle of the Coral Sea, Lieutenant McCuskey distinguished himself by fighting off *Zeros* that were trying to attack American torpedo planes. *Zeros* were shot down, while the torpedo planes went on to blast their target.

BEFORE THE WAR CAME TO GUADALCANAL

THE CORAL SEA action was brought on by a Japanese push into the Solomon Islands. The enemy was moving down the line of that archipelago northeast of Australia. American forces struck at the advance, and after a series of preliminary blows, the main battle developed. In one incident of the preliminaries the *Lexington* sent planes to blast the Japanese in the Solomon Island harbor of Tulagi, which they had just seized, and which we were to take from them several months later in the famous Solomon Island offensive launched by the Marines.

One of the pilots in the Tulagi raid was Lieutenant Elbert

Scott McCuskey of Arkansas. He was cited for the part he played in the bombing of a transport and a destroyer, the warship heavily battered, its guns silenced. The air squadron was on its way back when McCuskey's plane and another were forced down at sea.

They were not far from the shore of an island, and in their rubber boats got ashore. That island was Guadalcanal, not then known to fame: hardly known at all. A few months later Guadalcanal would flame into the news as an epic battlefield for Marines versus Japanese, but when McCuskey and his comrade landed on its shore, Guadalcanal was just another South Sea island, and there was no one to greet them but the fuzzy-wuzzy natives.

The two pilots were confronted by a sight more fearsome to them than any Japanese: black fellows armed with war clubs, stone axes, and human thigh bones shaped into knives. They looked like the hungriest of cannibals ready to dine on aviators. Appearances were deceptive. The natives were friendly, and offered their tribal hospitality.

With sign language the two Americans indicated that they wanted a fire built. The natives obliged readily. The fire making was accomplished in the primitive way, by rapidly revolving a stick inserted in the hole of another piece of wood. Then the two pilots used the blaze to signal at night. They had flashed radio word of their forced landings, and knew that a destroyer would be sent for them. Using a parachute to screen the fire on the side toward the sea, they flashed light signals in Morse code. When the destroyer they expected arrived, their improvised signal system directed it in. A cordial parting with their fuzzy-wuzzy friends, and good-by to Guadalcanal.

The battle of the Coral Sea began several days later. McCuskey played his big part on the second day, when he was one of the fighters escorting torpedo planes. Four Zeros ganged him. He shot one down, and engaged the other three in a wild scrimmage that kept them away from the torpedo planes while these blasted a Japanese carrier.

After the *Lexington* found a warrior's grave in the depths

of the Coral Sea, McCuskey went on to the *Yorktown* and the Battle of Midway. Once again he served on a carrier that destroyed Japanese flat-tops and then sank under enemy attack, fighting to the end.

At Midway McCuskey's plane was one of four that engaged eighteen Japanese dive bombers with a heavy escort of fighters. He shot down three dive bombers and damaged three others before his ammunition ran out. Later in the day he shot down two Zeros.

Weeks later McCuskey heard news that must have made him gasp: Guadalcanal, the headlines telling of the American landing and battle on that island which the war flyer of the Coral Sea and Midway could remember so well. One can imagine how McCuskey's thoughts must have drifted back to that tropical shore to which he went in his rubber boat. Then he had never suspected that the island on which he had a castaway's adventure would become front page in the news for months: the name of Guadalcanal writ large on the pages of history. McCuskey, more than most others, could visualize the Marines on that shore where he had seen the black welcoming committee with war clubs, stone axes, and knives made of human thigh bones. To him they had appeared, though deceptively, to be as fierce as the Japanese with whom the Marines were fighting in a battle to the death.

LIEUTENANT JOHN JAMES POWERS, U.S.N. (Missing) New York, New York
Congressional Medal of Honor

The destruction of a Japanese carrier of the *Shokako* class. You can see a bomb hit on the deck, and flame bursts from the bow. Lieutenant Powers gave his life in his determination to score a square hit, bombing from the lowest altitude to make sure.

THE FINEST CITATION OF ALL

REMEMBER, the folks back home are counting on us. I'm going to get a hit, if I have to lay it on their flight deck," said Lieutenant John James Powers, U.S.N., to his comrade flyers during the Battle of the Coral Sea.

Lieutenant Powers, commanding a formation of dive bombers, ordered to attack a Japanese carrier, fulfilled his resolve to place a bomb square on the enemy flight deck. This he did, and gave his life.

He led his dive bombers to the attack from an altitude of eighteen thousand feet. On the way down space was filled with antiaircraft fire and Japanese fighter planes. Powers plunged straight toward the deck of the carrier, until it was within five hundred feet of it. At that low level he discharged his seven-hundred-pound bomb.

He knew that a thousand feet of altitude was the minimum, if his plane was to be safe from explosion of its own bomb. That meant release the bomb at a thousand feet, so as to be able to pull out of the dive at seven hundred. But Powers bombed at five hundred feet, and pulled out at two hundred. He was last seen leveling off in an eruption of antiaircraft shells, bomb fragments, smoke, flame, and debris. "His plane was destroyed by the explosion of his own bomb," says the citation.

The official report tells with military factuality what a comrade relates with simple and affecting eloquence. John Nielsen was a pal of the superb flyer who, in the fraternity of pilots, was called Jo-Jo. He writes to Lieutenant Powers' mother, addressing her: "Dear Mother Powers." He explains: "I call you 'Mother Powers' because Jo-Jo used to call my mother 'Mother Nielsen.' My mother just idolized him."

The letter continues: "Jo-Jo was the best liked officer on the *Yorktown*. To both officers and men he represented the most perfect example of what a naval officer should be, and the kind so few of us are. I have never heard anyone speak anything but the best of him.

"So that you will know and forever be proud of your gallant son," Nielsen writes, "I'll tell you the story of his last attack against the enemy. The story of his gallantry and invincible spirit will live as long as this democracy shall continue to exist. On that morning, as we left the ready room to take off on the attack, Jo-Jo said to us all: 'I am going to get a hit, if I have to lay it on their flight deck. Remember, the folks back home are counting on us.'

"When we arrived over the target, and just before I pushed over in my dive, I glanced around at Jo-Jo, who was sitting just a few feet beyond my wing tip. He waved to me and grinned. When I pulled out of the bottom of my dive I looked around and saw Jo-Jo's plane directly over the center of the carrier at about three hundred feet. The last I saw, his plane was entering the column of smoke and debris over the target. He had dropped to a low altitude to make sure of getting an effective hit. Jo-Jo well knew and realized the dangers of a low pull-out, as he explained to us many times. But to a man of his caliber, thoughts of personal safety never occurred."

The finest citation of all, the letter to a mother from her son's best friend.

President Roosevelt told the American public of the heroic incident, and quoted Lieutenant Powers' words as a slogan for the American fighting forces: "Remember, the folks back home are counting on us."

Early in the war we heard much about Japanese suicide planes, a huge legend of how enemy flyers were only too eager to immolate themselves as a sacrifice to their Emperor. This was largely a myth, though apparently there have been cases of Japanese pilots deliberately trying to crash on American decks with exploding cargoes of bombs. In most of these cases it would appear that the Japanese plane had been hit badly, the pilot knew he was a goner anyway, and figured he might as well do as much damage to the hostile ship as he could. Any fighting man might reason that way. In the history of war you'll find repeated incidents of cornered soldiers resolved to sell their lives as dearly as possible.

Suicide bombing is not the American way. A United States war flyer is likely to take the most desperate chances, and go winging into a focus of danger where the chances are a thousand to one against him. His purpose is not self-immolation, but the destruction of the enemy. He is utterly resolved on hitting his objective, and never mind the risk. His mind and will are concentrated on the target, and if he does not come out alive, that is part of the game. He is capable of sacrificing himself if he sees a chance of inflicting a maximum blow upon the enemy, but he has the aggressive spirit of the warrior and not the resignation and an acceptance of doom that we attribute to oriental fatalism.

This is exemplified in the highest way in the story of Lieutenant

Powers, who waved and grinned as he dived to deliver a bombing attack at the lowest kind of level. He was trusting to his luck to come out of the desperate peril to which he was going, but, at the same time, he was willing to give his life if that were necessary in making absolutely certain of a square hit on the deck of the Jap carrier. It's no wonder the Japanese were beaten, their fleet shattered, when they had to contend with that kind of human element in the equation of war. Their own type of fatalism cannot match it. They will lose lives without accomplishing commensurate results. Already we hear that their front line of crack pilots have been wiped out in tactics of futile desperation.

PART SEVEN

THE BATTLE OF MIDWAY

MAJOR LOFTON R. HENDERSON, U.S.M.C. (Deceased), Coronado, California
Navy Cross

Solemn funeral rites for heroes of the Battle of Midway. One of the greatest of these was Major Lofton R. Henderson, who plunged his plane and load of bombs down the smokestack of a Japanese carrier.

THE SUPREME SACRIFICE

THE BATTLE OF MIDWAY was a three-day engagement, so far flung and complex that many of its details are still not known. There were two phases. One was fairly simple. The intricate maze of action and counteraction was to be found in the other.

The simple phase was an air blow against Midway Island. A huge Japanese invasion fleet steamed toward Hawaii, and a swarm of enemy planes flew to assault the outpost island, our advance base, Midway. The enemy plan was to smash the airfield, and thereby free themselves from land based planes flying from the island. The Midway defenders, with Marine Corps fighting planes bearing the brunt of the fight, gave the Japanese air fleet a fiery reception. Marine Corps pilots fought hostile bombers and fighters all over the sky, and shot down forty. Some bombing formations got through, and struck Midway. They inflicted serious damage, but failed to put the island base out of commission.

The immense complications of battle are found in air operations against the invasion fleet, a series of assaults by land based planes and by units of the fleet hurling air blows. Squadrons of heavy bombers, medium bombers, light bombers, and torpedo planes wove patterns of crisscross assault. The Japanese assailed our ships with their own carrier based aviation. There was almost no counting the attacks, the weaving flights of offensive maneuver, and the clash of planes in combat over great spaces of the sea.

The Japanese lost four aircraft carriers. We lost one, the *Yorktown*. A great number of other enemy ships were battered—two heavy cruisers and a light cruiser sunk, three battleships heavily damaged by bomb and torpedo hits. These losses mentioned are only examples of the havoc wrought upon the immense invasion fleet that was steaming toward Hawaii.

The American air assaults were signalized by exploits of the most spectacular valor. One of these was the deliberate diving of an American bomber into a Jap carrier. The pilot, who thus immolated himself was Major Lofton R. Henderson of Coronado, California.

Major Henderson was the commander of a dive bomber squadron based on Midway. They flew through a swarm of Zeros and into a blaze of antiaircraft fire, and blasted a carrier. Only half of their planes returned. Major Henderson led the assault. His supreme sacrifice was witnessed at close range by Corporal Eugene T. Card, of Oakland, California. Corporal Card, who was wounded three times, was a gunner in a bomber that was within three hundred feet of Major Henderson when he swooped down on the Jap carrier for his attack.

His plane was hit by Zeros or by antiaircraft fire, and was set afire. The dive bomber trailed a heavy stream of smoke as down it swooped. Major Henderson made no attempt to bail out, nor did he release his bombs when within bombing distance. There is no doubt but what his act was deliberate. He knew that in his burning plane he was doomed, and guided it for a headlong crash into the carrier. Corporal Card says he is certain that Major Henderson plunged his plane and its load of bombs down the smokestack of the carrier, and thus perished in one of the most fearsome deeds of war.

Thereby Major Lofton R. Henderson immortalized his name. Will it ever be forgotten? Hardly. Not as long as history retains the record of this global war. Will Henderson Field be forgotten? That Japanese air base which was seized and so bravely defended by the Marines on Guadalcanal was renamed in honor of the Marine Corps flyer who sacrificed himself in the destruction of an enemy carrier at Midway.

CAPTAIN RICHARD FLEMING, U.S.M.C. (Deceased), St. Paul, Minnesota
Congressional Medal of Honor

Like a fantastic caricature of a ship, a mighty Japanese vessel of war, after having been bombed by American carrier planes. Captain Fleming dedicated himself to bombing at such low level that it was almost certain to be fatal, and thereby gave his life.

HEROISM BY CALM DELIBERATION

IN POINT OF personality alone, Fleming of the Marines would have deserved a chapter in a book of personalities. He was half Irish and half French: his father an Irishman from England, his mother a member of a Nebraska French family. He cut a figure that held the eye: tall and lean, six feet two, dark haired and dark eyed, flashingly intelligent of eye, affable of manner, debonair, smiling. His easy-going courtesy made him immensely popular with his comrades.

Richard Fleming was a brilliant student in school, mentally avid, scholarly by temperament. His tastes ran toward things

[171]

of intellect and art; in particular, oddly enough, Japanese art. One of his closest friends was a Japanese merchant of St. Paul, with whom he liked to confabulate on matters of oriental philosophy and esthetics. From this Japanese friend he obtained treasures of a kind that he prized: rare oriental pipes. His hobby was the collection of pipes, of which he had a notable display.

His brother, Ward Fleming, was an aviation enthusiast, but Richard Fleming as a boy hardly thought about flying. He was without the usual winged fancy for airplanes so common in the young. Then why did he become a pilot? It was on an impulse of the moment. A friend who was to take his physical examination for air service in the Marines, asked Fleming to go along. Fleming did, and thought suddenly that he too would take the examination. He passed it, carried through with the thought he might as well enlist, and was on his way to adventure in the sky. In Marine Corps flight training he showed up so badly that he thought he would flunk out, but went on to become a brilliant pilot.

Such was the picture of Fleming, gifted, sensitive, artistic, and impulsive. Yet there was nothing impulsive about his deeds at Midway. He distinguished himself, and met his end in low level bombing attacks right on top of his targets. He swooped down into the most desperate of peril to make sure of bomb hits. But this was not rashness in the heat of battle. Before taking off for his assaults, Fleming carefully adjusted the mechanism of his bombs for release at the lowest levels.

On the first day at Midway he was with the dive bombers that flew from the island base. His was one of the planes that shattered and sank one of the four carriers the enemy lost in the battle.

Fleming, diving to the attack, was in the vortex of shells and bullets from Japanese fighter planes and from the antiaircraft batteries of the flat-top. He was in the concentrated fire all the way down to the level from which he bombed. That level was four hundred feet, although fifteen hundred feet was considered the minimum for safe bombing.

Diving to that almost suicidal four-hundred-foot level, his

plane was riddled by a hundred and seventy-nine bullets and shells, and he himself was wounded twice—minor injuries. He released his bombs for square hits on the carrier. At four hundred feet the odds were that his plane would be smashed by the explosion of its own bombs. But Fleming came out of it, and brought his damaged plane back to the carrier.

On the second day at Midway, Fleming was out to repeat his performance. Once again he adjusted his high explosive missiles for the lowest level of bombing. It was to be his last day. Fate had his number up. But then he always prepared himself as if any day of peril were to be his last. He was a devout Catholic, and made his confession and received Holy Communion before taking off.

This time his squadron assaulted a battleship. The enemy fire was so intense that dive bombing even from the orthodox fifteen hundred feet was an heroic exploit, but Fleming pressed on down to the extremely low level upon which he had resolved. His plane was hit repeatedly, and set on fire. It was blazing doom for Fleming, but he thought only of bombing. His comrades saw his burning plane release its high explosive at five hundred feet. He scored a near miss at the stern of the battleship, and crashed into the sea in flames.

Such was the end of the brilliant, impulsive Fleming, whose desperate tactics in dive bombing were coldly deliberate.

ENSIGN GEORGE H. GAY, U.S.N.R., Houston, Texas
Ensign Gay standing on the wing of Lieutenant McCuskey's plane. Seven Rising Suns
signify seven enemy planes shot down.

Torpedo Squadron 8, which sacrificed itself to American victory at Midway. Those airmen flew in a mighty American attack that destroyed three carriers. Of Squadron 8, not one plane returned, and only one man survived, Ensign G. H. Gay. All the other fifteen died in the unrelenting attack. *Standing left to right:* Lieutenant J. G. Owens, Jr., Ensign Fayle, John C. Waldron, R. A. Moore, U. M. Moore, W. R. Evans, G. W. Teats, H. J. Ellison. *Kneeling left to right:* G. M. Campbell, W. W. Ambercrombie, H. R. Kenyon, Jr., Ensign G. H. Gay, J. D. Woodson, W. W. Creamer, R. B. Miles

TORPEDO SQUADRON 8

THE INCREDIBLE adventure of Midway was that of Ensign George Henry Gay of Texas. The headlines told how he, while floating on the ocean, had a close-up view of the blasting of Japanese aircraft carriers, the destruction of which was a number-one feature of the American triumph. Ensign Gay had an experience such as no other man has ever approached.

He was a member of Torpedo Squadron 8, which earned immortal glory. This was the formation of torpedo planes that flew to attack a Jap carrier force, and played a dominant part in the sinking of those flat-tops. Not one plane returned and only one man, Ensign Gay. Prime Minister Churchill of Great Britain spoke stately words paying homage to the heroism and sacrifice of Squadron 8, which was later reconstituted and flew on to new renown.

In the whirl of battle at Midway the torpedo planes took off from their carrier to assail warships over the horizon. When the flyers came in sight of the enemy, they saw three carriers, two large ones and a small one. One of the big ones was burning, having been hit in an earlier attack. Torpedo Squadron 8 flew low to deliver another blow of devastation. An inferno of antiaircraft fire met them, and Jap fighter planes swooped down on them. But they pressed their attack in the face of certain destruction.

As Ensign Gay leveled off for his torpedo run, he heard his machine gunner say he had been hit. Gay kept on. Ahead was a great carrier of the *Kaga* class, and at this mighty target he launched his torpedo. That done, he swung his plane sharply to get away. A *Zero* was after him, and a shell from the Japanese fighter hit the rudder controls and smashed them. At the same time, a bullet hit Gay in the upper left arm.

The plane was mortally stricken. With the rudder mechanism out of action, it couldn't be controlled. The pilot could only land on the sea, which he did with clever pancaking tactics.

The gunner who had been hit during the approach to the carrier was dead. The plane sank, and carried with it the radio man, who could not get free. The pilot was able to clamber out, and found himself in the water. He had nothing with which to save himself, nothing but luck.

Up to the surface, as the plane plunged to the bottom, came a rubber boat, deflated. With it appeared a cushion, the kind on which the bombardier kneels while discharging his missile. Gay collected the rubber boat and the cushion. He could have inflated the boat with gas from the carbon monoxide bottle he had, and could have ridden comfortably in the life-saving craft. But Jap fighter pilots were known to machine-gun American aviators in rubber boats.

Gay had no desire to feel Japanese lead, and was even

afraid that Japanese pilots might see his head bobbing in the water. He used the cushion to conceal himself, ducked under it. Handling himself cleverly in the water, he was able to keep afloat under the concealment of the cushion and to have a view of what happened near by, a "fisheye" view.

He could see the three Japanese carriers easily. Torpedoes from Squadron 8 had hit them and damaged them heavily. Then Gay saw American dive bombers flashing into view, speeding down. Gay had a close-up vision of the stupendous drama of aerial attack. Bombs hit the Jap carriers. Masses of flame burst from them, and immense columns of smoke swirled skyward. Internal explosions shook and shattered the enemy flat-tops.

Ensign Gay had a fisheye view of it all, and as the hours of the afternoon wore on he saw Jap warships move survivors. One of the big carriers was blazing from stem to stern. He saw Japanese guns fire into the burning derelict to sink it, and enemy planes bombed it.

When night came Gay inflated the rubber lifeboat, got aboard, and drifted in the darkness. Next morning the Japanese were gone, their ships in fast retreat. An American naval plane came winging and spotted him. He was picked up, taken back to his carrier, and was able to report that of the carrier force of three one twenty-seven-thousand ton flat-top of the *Kaga* class was a certain loss, while the other big one and the smaller one were probable losses. Gay was decorated with the Navy Cross, as were all the others of Torpedo Squadron 8, posthumously.

LIEUTENANT COMMANDER CHARLES E. PERKINS, U.S.N., Wendell, North Carolina
Navy Cross

A naval observation plane procured this air picture of the result of a bombing raid against the Japanese at Kiska—the transport burning. Lieutenant Commander Charles E. Perkins and Lieutenant Lucius B. Campbell were decorated for heroic observation flying under the difficult conditions of the Aleutians—northern sea and craggy islands.

THE HEROISM OF GETTING THE FACTS

AERIAL DOGFIGHTS between lightning-paced fighters, smashing bombings of the enemy's industrial centers—the fighters and bombers make most of the headlines of the air war. Yet consider, for a moment, the lonely observation flight. It's clear enough that observation patrol work, the location of the enemy and the determination of his movements, is of the utmost importance. Yes, patrol work can be heroic, and nowhere more so than in the Aleutian Islands.

There weather conditions make aerial observation extremely difficult. Eternally shrouded by fog and blizzard, the Aleutians make an excellent hiding place for an enemy. It takes air scouting to spot him, and observation is possible only at short intervals and with great danger to pilot and crew. Flying, which always depends greatly on the weather, is here not a question of moonlit nights and cloud formation but the problem of taking off at all under a perpetual ceiling zero.

When the Japanese attacked the Aleutian Islands, while the Battle of Midway was being fought far to the south, laurels were earned by Patwing Four, meaning Patrol Wing Number Four. Flying from our Aleutian bases, Patwing Four operated against the Japs at Kiska. Its planes were the big long-range Catalina flying boats, intended only for observation—but the men of Patwing Four loaded the planes with high explosive and converted them into bombers.

The Navy Cross was awarded to Lieutenant Commander Charles E. Perkins of Wendell, North Carolina, for his heroic action in patrol in the Aleutians. His citation also reveals that Lieutenant Commander Perkins, piloting a Catalina patrol flying boat, bombed the Japs at Kiska Harbor in the face of a hurricane of antiaircraft fire but the main emphasis of the award is on an exploit that happened on patrol.

The big flying boat, with Perkins of North Carolina at the controls, was winging over enemy water, alone, without fighter escort. The sea below was gray and grim, then ahead through wisps of mist appeared several ships of a Japanese squadron. That was all important information. It meant enemy naval action pending—an attempt to land reinforcements or clear the waters around the Aleutians. Perkins flashed a report to headquarters and then flew on toward the warships. He wanted to find out more about them; every fact was of consequence to our own forces. The weather, as usual, was hazy, and he had to go below to spot the ships—to see just what type and in what strength.

The Japs opened with every antiaircraft gun they could bring to bear. The big Catalina flew through a sky punctured with lead. But Perkins stuck to his job. He hung grimly to the enemy naval forces until he had gleaned every bit of information that air observation could supply. Then he was able to inform our own striking forces of a powerful fleet of Japanese carriers, and signaled directions to guide an attack against the enemy.

That was the kind of individual action which time and again in the war of the Pacific proceeded a clash of warships on the sea. Victories for American squadrons in widely concerted actions were made possible by the daring of single flyers who, on solitary missions, swept the sea and flashed the intelligence without which the naval forces could not operate. In no case was braver work done than in the Aleutians, where the planes that Patwing Four flew on their patrol jobs traversing the most accursed skies on earth. Decorations were earned and received, as in the case of Lieutenant Commander Perkins.

The Navy Cross was awarded likewise to Lieutenant Lucius B. Campbell of Seattle. His citation, too, concerns patrol work. In a Catalina flying boat the airman from Seattle was flying in a dense snowstorm—Aleutian weather at its worst. He was near Umnak Island. South of that bleak bit of northern land he spotted enemy ships, a heavy concentration. Campbell set out to find all he could about them.

The weather was not his only worry, for he soon faced fighter opposition. Jap Zeros took off and zoomed around him, and a patrol plane is no powerfully armed Flying Fortress. Bullets ripped through the wings and fuselage, but Campbell dodged the Jap ships, finding out all he could about them, and signaling the information back to the American bases.

He stuck to it so long that he ran out of gas. Forced down at sea, when not another drop of fuel was left to keep his motor running, he was picked up by an American rescue vessel: a number one hero of observation patrol.

The valor of Perkins and Campbell is an example of the work done by American flyers during the long, dreary months while our forces were marking time and mustering strength for a blow to oust the Japs from the Aleutians. Day after day, those atrocious days of Aleutian weather, the bombers hit the Japs at Kiska and Attu, destroying their installations and disrupting their arrangements, until we were ready to launch an offensive. Then that offensive came, the landings on Attu, and the battle in the Aleutians took a new turn. But that was in the second year of America's war.

In the story of the Aleutians we find once again an example of the general fact of how the American fighting men had to wage their battles with an insufficiency of equipment and paucity of supplies. When the Japs struck their first blow in the Northern Pacific, seizing outlying islands and bombing Dutch Harbor, we had only a minimum of equipment with which to beat them off. The bright side of the picture is the way masses of materiel and hosts of reinforcements did arrive for the operations of the second year: Uncle Sam rallying from his unpreparedness and piling up the weapons of war with all the immense resources of American industry.

PART EIGHT

GUADALCANAL

MAJOR GENERAL ALEXANDER A. VANDEGRIFT, U.S.M.C., Charlottesville, Virginia
Congressional Medal of Honor
Navy Cross
General Vandegrift is seen with Rear Admiral John S. McCain, who commanded the
United States naval air forces in the South Pacific—a meeting in the Solomon Islands.

The landing of the Marines in the Solomon Islands. Here they are forcing their way ashore on Florida Island. You can see the landing barges speeding toward land and others drawn up near the jungle shore. In the Solomons, the equatorial forest is dense and miasmal—the sweltering hell of the jungle.

VANDEGRIFT OF GUADALCANAL

A COMMANDING OFFICER of an important campaign may do a superb job and yet not have any particular occasion to display gallantry in action. He may have to exercise great qualities of moral courage and fortitude of mind, without having to take a personal part in the fighting. It is true that in this modern war a general is likely enough to ride a tank into the thick of the fray, and an admiral aboard his flagship may lead his column into a blazing engagement. But it is entirely possible for a commanding officer to fulfil his tasks in the most eminent way and never have the opportunity for a show of hardihood in a moment of danger.

[185]

It was entirely otherwise with Major General Alexander A. Vandegrift. His command embraced a major theater of war, and at the same time kept him in a place of constant danger. He was the Marine Corps chief at Guadalcanal, and every inch of ground that his Leathernecks held was a point of peril. His abilities as a military leader were demonstrated by the coordinated skill of the landing and by the adept tactics of the Marines in the long and desperate battles amid the jungles. He was constantly in the zone of hazard. Hazard was everywhere, and Vandegrift of the Marines was the sort of soldier whose impulse took him to the blazing corner where things were the hottest. The firing line was his natural habitat.

His citation for the Congressional Medal of Honor states all this with military brevity: "His courage and resourcefulness prevailed against a strong, determined and experienced enemy." And the citation speaks of "this dangerous but vital mission, accomplished at the constant risk of his life."

But then Vandegrift was used to danger. His long career had taken him to brewing caldrons of danger all around the world. The Marines always were a traveling lot, and he served on many a continent, island, and ocean. A mere list of the medals for bravery that he received gives hint of a whole book full of exciting exploits. He was among the many Marines who distinguished themselves in the Nicaraguan jungle war and in Haiti, where the perils were those of the most savage kind of terrain—mountain crags and equatorial forest; in Mexico—the landing under fire at Vera Cruz; along the Yangtze—with its memories of Chinese bandits and invading Japs.

The Vandegrift way of pushing into places where the bullets fly is illustrated by a wild few minutes at a jungle point on Guadalcanal. The Commander, with some others, was inspecting the fighting front. They stopped at a place infested by Japs. The enemy was lurking in the surrounding jungle, and suddenly they rushed the Vandegrift party.

"Three Japs surprised us," relates the General. "They came out of the woods yelling 'Banzai.' The leading Jap shot and killed my signal sergeant, and a sergeant major raised his rifle and shot and killed this Jap. A corporal near by aimed his pistol at a second Jap, but the pistol failed to go off. So he threw it at the Jap, at the same time making a flying tackle that hurled the Jap to the ground. When the corporal got up he found the Jap was dead—he had been shot, but I don't know by whom. The third Jap fled into the jungle with several Marines after him."

That was the kind of action which stormed more than once around the commander of the Marines during the memorable days of Guadalcanal. General Vandegrift displayed the personal courage in desperate combat which is a prime requisite in bestowing the Congressional Medal of Honor.

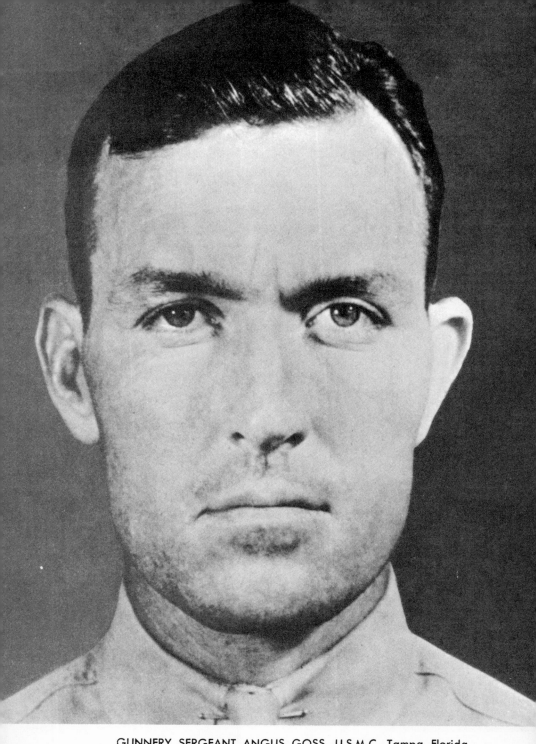

GUNNERY SERGEANT ANGUS GOSS, U.S.M.C., Tampa, Florida

MAJOR HARRY TORGERSON U.S.M.C., Valley Stream, Long Island

[189]

CORPORAL GEORGE F. GRADY, U.S.M.C. (Deceased), New York City

Tulagi Island, where the American landing was met by savage Japanese resistance. The enemy soldiers defended themselves ferociously in the hills, and took refuge in caves and cliffs, where they battled to the death. Sergeant Goss, Captain Torgerson (now Major) and Corporal Grady distinguished themselves in the ferocious struggle before the Japanese were wiped out.

BLASTING THE JAPANESE OUT OF THEIR HOLES

WHEN THE AMERICAN push into the Solomon Islands is mentioned, we think of Guadalcanal. That island witnessed a prolonged agony of human blood and jungle filth that culminated finally in the wiping out of the Japanese, with nothing left to show but the wreckage of equipment and the bloated foulness of rotting carcasses. But Guadalcanal was only one point of the original attack, only one island where the Marines landed. The offensive was a two-day affair, a double drive into the southern Solomons. One prong was thrust at Guadalcanal, while the other was aimed at the Florida Island area.

Guadalcanal was a large island and an important one, where the Japanese had nearly finished an elaborate landing field. The first landing of the Marines took them utterly by surprise, and they gave little resistance, scampering to the hills, fleeing to the jungles in order to snipe. The landing of the Marines on Guadalcanal was almost eventless—the fury of fighting began later.

The Florida Island area consists of a major island and some minor ones, the strategic importance of the group resting with the latter—Tulagi, Gavutu, and Tanambogo. Tulagi has a fine harbor and makes a good naval base. Gavutu and Tanambogo are small bits of land, just off Tulagi and near to each other—important for the control of Tulagi and its harbor.

The Marines' landing at Tulagi, Gavutu, and Tanambogo encountered ferocious resistance. The Japanese did not stop fighting until they were ripped to ribbons and blown into fragments. It was a death struggle, hand to hand, knife to knife, hand grenade against hand grenade, men obsessed with the fury to kill—striking, shooting and slashing to the last breath.

The three islands of Tulagi, Gavutu, and Tanambogo are mountainous—the Solomons consisting largely of mountain tops thrust above the surface of the sea. Crags and summits are interspersed with jungle, the malarial fantasy of the equatorial forest, terrain well suited for the kind of defense the Japanese knew so well—trained as they were to jungle fighting. They were veterans, too, troops inured to war, long practiced in the art of inflicting violent death, seasoned in battle in China, in the Philippines, and the Dutch East Indies. They were experienced in the tactics of infiltrating behind lines in the treacherous gloom of the tropical thicket. Yes, the Japanese knew their murderous business.

Of the Marines the majority were boys who had never seen a shot fired to kill. They had had their battle schooling at Parris Island or on the West Coast, and were ready, fit, tough of body and spirit. But they were, when all is said and done, typical American youths who had been given the routine Marine training. Now, for their first fight, they stormed into a hell hole manned by the veteran jungle fighters of Japan.

They ripped the Japs apart, outslugged them at their own game, outmaneuvered them, outfought them, outdid them in their own practiced trade of slaughter. No prisoners were taken at Tulagi, Gavutu, and Tanambogo. Not a Jap was left. The embittered enemy fought until he was a corpse, fought with unyielding fury, with no thought but killing and dying.

Weirdest of all was the cave fighting. The craggy islands are covered with limestone cliffs, and into these the Japs had tunneled, making cliffside dugouts, small caves for defense. When the Marines forced their landings, the Japs retired to these caves, shooting from them, hurling hand grenades. They battled to the end, dying in their caves to the last man. The Marines exterminated them with hand grenades, tossing high explosive into the entrances of the tunnels—until crowded caves were turned into charnel houses littered with mangled, shattered Japanese.

Gunnery Sergeant Angus Goss of Tampa, Florida, was an expert with explosives; he had instructed classes in firing mortars, and had qualified with the engineering branch of the Marine Corps as an expert at demolition work. So Sergeant Goss knew all about tossing hand grenades into a Jap tunnel. The one he picked on Tulagi Island was the toughest of all, and a grim competition with death ensued.

Sergeant Goss hurled a hand grenade into the cave, but it came right back at him; before it could explode, a Jap picked it and returned the favor. The Sergeant threw another grenade, and again it came back at him. This continued—as fast as the Sergeant threw his missiles into the cave, the Japanese tossed them out.

The Sergeant, wise to the ways of grenades, tried a trick. The Japanese inside were having too much time before the explosive went off. So he pulled the pin of a grenade, and held it for three seconds before tossing it. After that interval it went off almost as soon as it was thrown inside the cave. Yet a Japanese was quick enough to get this one too and throw it out. The Sergeant tried his second trick several times, but it was no go.

Some other means had to be found to obliterate the Japanese in the cave, and it wasn't hard for the demolition expert to think of something else. He took a big charge of TNT—enough high explosive to rip the cave apart—and pushed it into the tunnel to explode. The Japanese pushed out the TNT, and it blew up outside. This time the Sergeant got hurt, the bursting charge driving splinters into his legs.

The Sergeant got mad. Under ordinary circumstances he was willing to do things in an orthodox way, but the pain in his legs burned away all restraint. He picked up a tommy gun and plunged into the cave, blazing away. He killed four Japanese, all that remained alive. There were eight more Japs in the cave —dead—killed in previous fighting.

On Gavutu Island the champion cave blaster was Captain Harold L. Torgerson of Valley Stream, Long Island. There was nothing so scientific about Torgerson's tactics. His method was that of brute force—the brute force of dynamite and lots of it. He would string sticks of dynamite together, as many as thirty, and make his way to a tunnel entrance. To keep the Japanese inside from interfering, four Marines with rifles and machine guns would blaze away, peppering the cave mouth with a stream of bullets. Then into the tunnel Torgerson would push his string of thirty-six sticks of dynamite and light the fuse.

He had some narrow escapes. An enemy bullet carried away his wristwatch. Another hit him in the seat of the pants. Several times he was barely able to get away from the explosion of his own dynamite.

The most memorable blast was when he tied a five-gallon can of gasoline to a string of thirty sticks of dynamite. That would make it a really fancy blowup. But the result almost spelled the end of Torgerson. Dynamite and gasoline went off with a shattering repercussion and sheets of flame. The blast knocked Torgerson down and blew his trousers completely off.

A champion Japanese killer on Gavutu was Corporal George F. Grady, who gave his life to destroy Japs. This is a story of brothers. He was one of five Gradys who grew up in Manhattan, typical lads of the Irish West Side. Three of the five Gradys went to war. The youngest, Stephen, is a Marine Corps paratrooper, following in the footsteps of George—who likewise was a

Leatherneck parachutist. It was tough for Stephen, when he joined up; George had made a fine record as a soldier. As Stephen wrote home: "These damn instructors sure rub it in, being that I'm George's brother. You should hear the way they praise him. They say he is the best damn soldier you've ever seen."

Martin Grady is listed as missing in action—a sergeant of the Marine Air Force. He was at Hickam Field, Pearl Harbor, when the Japanese struck on December 7. He flew in the Solomons, and took part in the operations over Gavutu, playing his part in the bombing and strafing that accompanied the island fighting in which his brother was killed. Martin Grady flew in air battles until he was reported missing in action.

George Grady is described as the mildest of brothers, quiet, studious. He had served a four-year hitch in the Marines when the war came, and when he was ready to leave for combat in the Southwestern Pacific, his remark at home was: "I wonder how it is going to feel to kill somebody."

The island of Gavutu is little more than a hill, the tip of a mountain sticking above the water. Steep slopes confronted the Marines when they landed, and it was upgrade work as they sought the enemy. The Japanese were in strongly placed positions, shooting and sniping. The Marines stalked them, rushed them, shooting with rifle and pistol, slashing with bayonet and knife. George Grady charged an entrenched group of eight Japanese. Working his way in close, he got into position to blast them with a sub-machine gun. His gun spat fire, and two Japs dropped. Then the gun jammed. He plucked at the trigger; nothing happened—nothing but the ghastly ineffectuality of a gun that won't shoot. Grady might have ducked away to safety, but the lust to kill Japanese was fierce in him, the primeval instinct to destroy the enemy. He leaped forward, swinging the gun as a club. He smashed down one Jap, killing him with a bludgeoning blow, then dropped his gun and reached to his belt and whipped out his sheath knife. He lunged at a Jap, killing him with a slash. He leaped upon another, sinking the knife to the hilt. He slaughtered five of the eight Japs, but the other three were on him, and George died as he slashed.

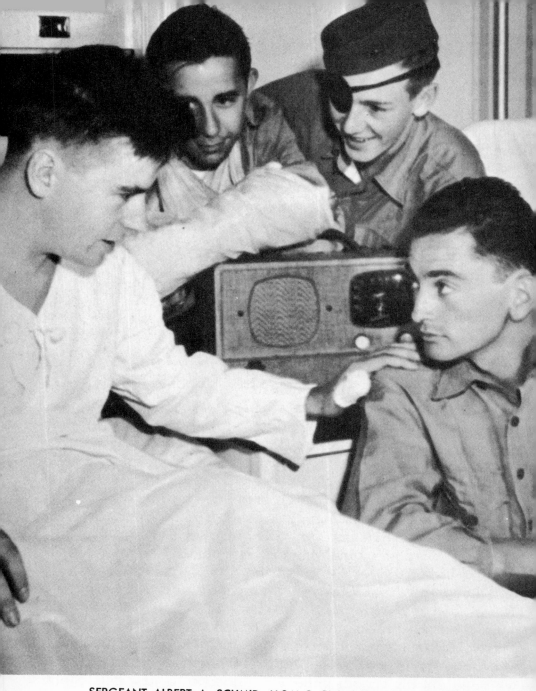

SERGEANT ALBERT A. SCHMID, U.S.M.C., Philadelphia, Pennsylvania
Navy Cross

Sergeant Schmid, in a hospital bed, is seen talking things over with Corporal LeRoy
Diamond, his foxhole companion in the Battle of the Tenaru River.

More than 200 Japs were killed as they tried to cross the Tenaru River in the face of Schmid's machine-gun fire. He mowed down waves of them before he was blinded by an exploding hand grenade.

THE BATTLE OF TENARU RIVER

THE MARINE LANDING on Guadalcanal in August took the Japanese by complete surprise, and the Leathernecks encountered no real opposition. Having seized the airfield the enemy had constructed, they dug in and waited. They knew that other parts of the jungle island swarmed with Japanese and that they were outnumbered ten to one. The enemy was sure sooner or later to stage a big push, an all-out attempt to smash the Marines based on Henderson Field. That attempt came on August 21, when the battle of Tenaru River was fought.

The contending forces faced each other across the river. The

American positions along one bank consisted of a series of machine-gun nests, each a hole with a gun crew. In one of these nests the gunner was Johnny Rivers, a Philadelphia lad who had started out as a professional boxer before he joined the Leathernecks. The loader for his gun was Private Albert Schmid of Philadelphia. A third man in the hole was Lee Diamond of New York. The time was night, and a great tropical moon was shining.

Suddenly a few shots were fired from across the river. Then a dark mass came lunging down the opposite bank and into the water like a milling herd of cattle fording a stream. The river there was fifty yards wide and easy to wade.

"No you don't, not tonight," whispered a voice in the American machine-gun nest.

The machine gun spat fire. Johnny Rivers swept it to and fro. In the bright moonlight he couldn't miss, and wading Japs crumpled into the water.

There was a storm of enemy fire, and Johnny Rivers fell across his gun—drilled by a bullet. They laid him to one side, and gun loader Al Schmid took his place, the loading now being done by the third man, Lee Diamond. The Japanese continued their charge across the stream. Groups of from thirty to fifty lunged down into the moonlit stream and came floundering across. Al Schmid swept his gun evenly across one group after another, and the Japs toppled over each other.

As he was loading cartridge belts, Lee Diamond was hit and fell across the gunner's legs. He was gravely wounded. Schmid laid him aside, and did his own loading. As the Japanese kept coming, he actually snapped in cartridge belts and fired.

The stubborn machine-gun post was a mark for a concentrated attack. Japanese filtered across the river upstream and downstream, and worked their way close to snipe. Some were shooting from high up in the treetops. Bullets were coming from all directions. They sang around the gunner's ears as he continued to operate the machine gun, holding the banks of the Tenaru.

Suddenly he felt that his chest was wet, drenched. Blood, he thought at first—but it was water. A fountain was spurting from the machine gun, the water jacket of which had been punctured by several bullets. That seemed the end of the machine-gun post, for Schmid had always been told that without water a gun in action would heat up, the metal would expand, and the gun would jam. He kept on shooting, and sure enough the barrel grew blistering hot in his hands. But it didn't jam. To Schmid's surprise, hot as it was, the gun kept on firing.

What happened next was told later by the Marine as follows: "I had just mowed down a particularly big party that came charging at us from across the stream, when all hell broke loose in our hole. What must have been a hand grenade hit the left stirrup of the machine gun and blasted it into junk."

How he escaped being killed was a miracle. The explosion of the grenade blew off the heavy bolt handle of the gun. Like a projectile it flew past Schmid's face, grazing his shoulder in its flight.

"My helmet was knocked off," Schmid said afterward. "Something struck me in the face. Everything became dark. I put my hand to my face and eyes. I felt blood and raw flesh. I strained my eyes hoping for a glimmer of light, but I couldn't see."

Lee Diamond, wounded as he was, tried to help his comrade, who was blinded and in agony. Schmid worked his right hand around and got out his forty-five.

Diamond cried: "Don't shoot, Smitty, don't shoot yourself."

Smitty laughed: "Don't think I'll do that. The first Jap that jumps in here will be on the receiving end of this forty-five."

"But you can't see."

"You tell me from which way he's coming and I'll try to get him."

The wounded men lay there for hours. Morning came. The enemy attack was gradually being rolled back. A lieutenant made his way to the machine-gun hole and gave Smitty a shot in the arm with a hypodermic needle to dull his pain. A private of the Medical Corps, braving a hail of bullets, brought water, poured it into a helmet, and put Smitty's face in it to drink.

Between eight and nine o'clock the two wounded men were taken out. The firing was dying down, the Japanese attack definitely beaten off. Smitty was credited with having killed more than two hundred Japs in the battle for the river crossing. His heroic gunnery had stopped the enemy at a vital point, and without it the American victory could hardly have been won. At the hospital the doctors found he had one eye blinded, forever sightless. The other was injured, but he was able to see. Back in the United States he was decorated with the Navy Cross, with the light of day entering the one eye that was left to the desperate fighter of Guadalcanal, whose escape from blindness had been as narrow as his escape from death.

Yes, and he married the girl who was waiting for him. Everywhere across the nation the press, with stories and pictures, featured the wedding of Smitty, who defended the ford of the river in that critical battle on Guadalcanal.

He, perhaps, more than any other represents the tenacity of the man in the foxhole—not the fury of the attack, not the excitement of the assault, but the iron and unrelenting temper of the machine gunner at his post. Any man from a battle front will tell you how supremely important one single machine gun can be, one weapon at a strategic point. If it can hold out, continue firing and keep the enemy back for a few desperate minutes more, the whole issue of the fight may be changed. Napoleon said that the army which resists for the last quarter of an hour wins the battle—and this historic maxim may be applied to that particular corner in the battle of the Tenaru River, the corner where Smitty and his machine gun held out for seemingly impossible hours.

Today we think of the Battle of Guadalcanal as an affair of wiping out the Japs, the Americans attacking, advancing, pursuing the enemy from one jungle haunt to another. That was the story during the final phases, but for a desperate while the task of the Marines was to defend. They had to hang on grimly and stoically, and fight off constant enemy attack. The Leathernecks needed all their tenacity, until the arrival of reinforcements and equipment turned the course of the fighting from the defensive to a surging assault. Then the Marines, who had held out so staunchly at Henderson Field, were able to give free rein to that other kind of Leatherneck courage—the dashing spirit of the advance that sweeps on. Thus Guadalcanal was won—the first bit of conquered land taken away from the Japs.

COLONEL MERRITT A. EDSON, U.S.M.C., Burlington, Vermont
Congressional Medal of Honor
Here Colonel Edson was decorated by Admiral Nimitz, Commander in Chief of the United
States Pacific fleet. At the left of Admiral Nimitz is Major General Vandegrift, Commander
of the Marines. And at the right of the picture is Brigadier General Rupertus of the Marine
Corps.

The ridge after the battle—the hillcrest where the Marine Corps raiders, under the command of Colonel Edson, killed 600 Japs in bitter fighting that repelled the enemy attack—thereby saving Henderson Field.

HE KNEW HIS JUNGLES

THERE IS AN interesting relation between Guadalcanal and Nicaragua, although the Solomon Islands and Central America are far apart indeed in point of space. But there are similarities. Both are jungle country, where battlefields are a fright, a fantasy of morass and tropical thicket. In the late twenties, the days of Sandino, the Marines campaigned in Nicaragua. Of Leatherneck bravery in the jungle fighting there was an abundance, and special medals were awarded for valor in Nicaragua.

Among the Marines on Guadalcanal were veterans of those Central American battles—and they knew the ways of war in

[203]

the equatorial forest. Take Colonel Edson, commander of the Marine Raider Battalion. He was Captain Edson in Nicaragua, and specialized in jungle tactics, of which the following is an example.

In one Nicaragua operation he was in command of a Marine patrol pushing through a bedeviling stretch of river country, advancing from the Coco River to the Poteca River. Hostile Nicaraguans—fighters of the insurgent forces led by the redoubtable Sandino—were all around them in force. The Marine patrol encountered superior numbers well entrenched along a river bank. The Leathernecks attacked. An advance guard dashed forward, its leader, Edson, out in front. The Nicaraguan position had to be stormed close up, in man-to-man fighting. He commanded the assault skilfully, and battled with the rest of his men in personal combat. He was both the tactician and an outstanding individual fighter in the violent action that drove a superior force from a strong position.

Of Edson's work in Nicaragua, his commanding officer wrote: "Captain Edson had demonstrated that when properly led, Marines can travel in the dry and rainy seasons. This has been done in the face of almost insurmountable obstacles, and far beyond the reach of supporting troops. During the three months that Captain Edson has served in Nicaragua he has spent ten months in the interior actively patrolling all trails and rivers." He was in twelve different clashes with hostile forces during that time.

In the Solomons Edson found work that must have reminded him forcibly of his Nicaraguan days fifteen years before. He was younger then, but middle age had not lessened the physical vigor or spiritual fortitude of the Marine Corps veteran. He had a fighting command in the bloody, mucky business that attended the seizure of Gavutu and Tanambogo Islands—his raider battalion playing a foremost part in the extermination of the Japanese, killing them virtually Jap by Jap. And in the ferocious battles on Guadalcanal Edson and the raiders reached the climax of gory action, as murderous a fight to the death as men have ever engaged in.

Five days after the landing and capture of Henderson Field, the raider battalion was ordered to storm a ridge of hills a thousand yards to the south—a ridge that dominated the surrounding jungle and was the key to the control of the field. The raiders, led by Edson, battled their way to the ridge, occupied it and dug in. They had some bitter fighting, but the capture of the ridge was the lesser part of it. The Japanese massed for a counter attack, and then came the raiders' supreme ordeal.

The enemy drove forward in superior numbers in a fanatical rage, wild with the lust to kill, hungry for slaughter. They broke through, and it looked as if disaster had overtaken Edson and his raiders. The situation was saved by the tactics of the commander, that skilful Edson way of handling troops in jungle fighting. With a deft maneuver he drew his men back at a critical point, establishing a reserve line. This surmounted the first crisis, but the second crisis was even more savage.

The Japs launched a series of ferocious assaults on the reserve line. They lurched forward with contorted faces, drunk with the homicidal mania that is instilled in the Japanese soldier. They looked like fiends and devils, as they came shooting and closed in stabbing. The Marines watched them in murderous hate, every man a killer—felling them with bullets, slashing them with bayonets, blowing them to pieces with grenades. The Japanese charged repeatedly, and it was a deadly hand-to-hand mêlée with rifles, bayonets, pistols, grenades and knives—a death grapple of shooting and slashing. The strategic ridge was a welter of dead men.

Colonel Edson of the Marine Raider Battalion was that same Captain Edson of the Leatherneck patrols in Nicaragua—mixing it with the enemy at points where the swirl of battle was the fiercest. Leadership and personal combat were the Edson secret. Fighting in the forefront, he held his men firmly in their positions until the Japanese attacks were beaten off. That is how the Americans retained possession of a jungle-dominating ridge of hills, the key to the control of Henderson Field. Today that line of hills is named Edson's Ridge.

PRIVATE HARRY DUNN, U.S.M.C., Springfield, Ohio
Navy Cross

Three Japs were killed by Private Dunn as he hid in the foxhole, after being cut off from his outfit. He got back to the American lines, carrying a wounded Marine Corps comrade on his back.

THE LOYALTY OF A MARINE

IF PRIVATE HARRY DUNN of the Marines had done no more than get back, he would have been a hero—but he brought a comrade back with him. In heavy fighting on Guadalcanal, he was isolated from a patrol detachment. It was night, and the Japs were all around him. In the darkness Harry Dunn took refuge in an empty Japanese foxhole. Parties of the enemies came searching. He fought them off. Twice during the night he exchanged shots with Japanese soldiers, and wounded or killed at least three.

When day came the Marine in the foxhole figured the game was up. Japanese appeared in large numbers. He played dead,

and got away with it. The Japanese stripped him of every bit of his equipment and left him lying there. They moved on, and Dunn figured he might have a chance to sneak through to his own lines, which were along a river.

He started out, and heard something—a sound from near by. It was the call of a wounded Marine, Private Jack Morrison. Dunn went to him and gave him first-aid; Morrison couldn't travel, and Dunn hated to think of his buddy falling into the hands of the Japanese. He picked up the wounded man, and carried him— Morrison on Dunn's back.

In that piggy-back fashion they got to the river. An enemy patrol spied the two, and opened fire. Dunn ducked into the brush, still carrying Morrison, and crawling through the dense thicket, evaded pursuit.

They remained hidden all day, and at night started out again, Morrison clinging to Dunn's back. Jap patrols appeared, making them move back to the brush. One patrol searched for them, but Dunn took himself and Morrison to safe concealment deep in the jungle along the river.

At dawn Marines on guard at the American fighting line saw a strange sight—a man staggering forward with another man on his back. The wounded Morrison was taken to a hospital for treatment. Dunn was carried to the hospital too, suffering from complete exhaustion.

Back in some American town you may see a couple of Marines keeping to themselves, talking with each other and pretty much ignoring the rest of the world. They're a rather exclusive tribe, those Leathernecks, and do not hobnob easily with other people, other uniforms. They're proud, even a bit aloof: and that's *esprit de corps*. They stick together, one for the other. Let a Marine get into a jam, and see how the others flock to his aid.

In war you'll find that same *esprit de corps* manifested in the way of battle: a Marine standing by a fellow Marine to the limit of human courage. In a tight corner of battle, he'll excel in the devoted task of getting a comrade out. The way the Marines will stick together was seen in superlative style when at a battle-

line on Guadalcanal a Marine staggered in carrying another Marine on his back. The Armed Forces place emphasis on the merit of that kind of courage, the steadfast loyalty of a fighting man toward his comrades. It is a binding tie of morale that redoubles the effectiveness of a military unit.

COAST GUARDSMAN DOUGLAS A. MUNRO (Deceased), South Cle Elum, Washington
Congressional Medal of Honor

COAST GUARDSMAN JAMES D. FOX, Uniontown, Pennsylvania

COXWAIN ROBERT J. CANAVAN, U.S.C.G., Chicago, Illinois

Supplies for fighting Leathernecks being unloaded on the beach of Guadalcanal Island. In the background may be seen part of the convoy that delivered the supplies.

THE COAST GUARD AT GUADALCANAL

THE PART PLAYED by the Coast Guardsmen in Guadalcanal has not been given sufficient publicity. Their boats were foremost in the landing of the Marines. Throughout the Battle of Guadalcanal they did hazardous work off the beaches, and at Henderson Field Coast Guardsmen braved the peril of the Japanese attack, joining in the fighting with rifle and machine gun.

Of all this a vivid picture abounding in lively episode was given by a Coast Guardsman from Guadalcanal on his return to the United States. He was machinist James D. Fox of Uniontown, Pa., nicknamed Sly Fox. There were three brothers-in-arms: Sly Fox; John Lydon of Louisville, Kentucky, who was called the "Big Irishman"; and Richard J. Scarsborough of Avon, North Carolina, whom they called "Scars." Sly Fox told how in the original landing, Coast Guardsmen worked for two days and nights without rest, getting Marines and supplies onto the beaches at Guadalcanal. Utterly worn out, they were told to take their boats offshore, drop anchor, and get their first night of sleep. As usual, the three musketeers were together, Sly Fox, Big Irishman Lydon, and Scars Sarsborough.

"We didn't get much sleep though," Sly Fox relates. "It was raining as hard as I've ever seen it come down, which made it mighty uncomfortable. Then, just as we were getting accustomed to the deluge, the Japanese fleet came in, and let go at our ships offshore. The battle lasted all night, the most terrific naval fight anyone ever saw." While it was as spectacular as a fireworks display, it was not very soothing, and that section offshore became known as "Sleepless Lagoon."

When the American camp was set up ashore at Henderson Field, Sly Fox, Big Irishman Lydon, and Scars Scarsborough were assigned to bunk with their commander, the Coast Guard officer in charge of all shore operations in the Solomons, Commander Dwight H. Dexter. Bunking with the Old Man might well be embarrassing for three enlisted men, might cramp their style and curb their animal spirits. And the Japanese added to the embarrassment.

Telling of their quarters, bunking with their commanding officer, Sly Fox relates: "It was a little house on stilts, and one day the Big Irishman, Scars and I were sitting round in a circle when the Japs started a fierce artillery barrage. Right off the bat a big chunk of shrapnel tore through the roof and crashed to the floor in the middle of us. If it had been one foot off in either direction, it would certainly have hit and probably killed one of us. 'We must have been wearing halos!' " says Sly.

The barrage was so fierce that all hands were ordered into shelter, and Sly Fox found himself in a big one with nine other men. At the thundering height of the bombardment one end of the dugout was hit, and caved in. They started to evacuate, getting out through the other end, which was open. One of the men had been knocked daffy by the blast, and refused to leave. Sly Fox grabbed him and dragged him out. A minute later another barrage came over and shattered the dugout shelter completely.

After bunking with their commander for a while, the three pals were assigned to a tent at Henderson Field. Sly Fox had a Japanese blanket, a trophy of war which he had picked up as a souvenir. One night he, Big Irishman Lydon and Scars Scarsborough were in the tent, when the Japs opened a barrage. They ducked out into a foxhole until the shelling was over, and when they returned they found the tent ventilated with seventy-two shrapnel holes. In the folded Japanese blanket was a hole, where a shell fragment had ripped through four layers.

Relating Guadalcanal stories, Sly Fox preferred to tell about the exploits of other Coast Guardsmen. He expressed a mighty admiration for Albert di Pasquale, fireman second class of Highland, New Jersey, who was so powerful that they called him the mighty *Di Pas*. Di Pas on one occasion manned a tank lighter all by himself. He handled the craft single-handed, doing the work of four men, and he did it under heavy fire.

"The Mighty Di Pas," said Sly Fox, "went native. He walked in his bare feet until they became as tough as leather, and he learned to climb trees for coconuts with the speed of a native."

Another prodigious fellow was Cockswain Robert J. Canavan of Chicago, who, without a life preserver, swam for nineteen hours—an almost superhuman feat of courage and endurance.

Canavan was in one of three Higgins landing boats that were cruising offshore on an antisubmarine patrol. Not much happened, until number three boat started on its way back to Guadalcanal. Canavan was in that one, and tells how all of a sudden they spied a light cruiser coming round a point of land. The warship flew no ensign, and the Coast Guardsmen were undecided about her nationality, but not for long. Their doubts were dispelled when the cruiser charged them with heavy machine-gun fire. There was no escape to shore on Guadalcanal. They were eight miles from land and the cruiser was between them and the coast. They tried to run for Tulagi. It was no go. The landing boat was being riddled by the guns of the armored warship. The men aboard realized their craft was done for, and went overboard: everyone but Canavan. The last man to go turned to him and yelled: "I'll see you in hell, Bob." Canavan still had a faint hope of getting the boat to shore and beaching it, and stuck to the stearing wheel, crouching and trying to navigate.

"When the Japs riddled the instrument panel and tore the wheel up," Canavan said later, "I figured it was time for me to leave. I had noticed that the others had worn their life jackets when they had gone over, and it occurred to me that they made mighty good targets. So I shed my jacket before I rolled off the gunwale. As I hit the water, a burst of gunfire ripped the floor boards where I had been kneeling.

"Floating on my back," Canavan went on, "I could see the cruiser as she passed within fifty feet of me. The Japs were dressed in whites and the bugle was sounding what was probably mess call. The Japs thought I was dead, and they didn't bother me, but continued on to where the rest of the crew were struggling in the water. When the cruiser reached them, she halted for about five minutes, and a sound of machine-gun fire came to me across the water. When she moved on, none of the boys were visible."

Canavan was nearer to Guadalcanal than to Tulagi, but there were strong currents and, if he had tried to swim to Guadalcanal, it would have taken him to a Japanese section of the shore. So Tulagi it had to be, and that was thirteen miles away. Moreover, its nearest point was being shelled by a Japanese destroyer, and Canavan didn't want to get anywhere near that ship. He lay floating until the destroyer had gone, and then he started to swim.

"At first," he relates, "I used the crawl, but later switched exclusively to the side and back strokes. They took less energy out of me. I hummed all the songs I knew, in an effort to keep my spirits up. Twice it rained heavily. Each time the sky darkened, and the sea got choppy. I did more praying in those hours I spent in the water than I had done in the twenty previous years of my life. Three times I gave up, and tried to drown myself, but didn't have the guts."

After nineteen hours of exposure in the water Canavan managed to beat his way to land. The shallows were jagged with sharp coral reefs, which cut his feet badly. He got to shore, bleeding and exhausted. Then he went looking for somebody, but found only natives. They seemed friendly but could not understand English, and he started traveling to find the Marines. He was trudging along the shore when he saw a boat-load of them passing. He yelled and waved frantically but could not attract their attention.

After toiling on for miles he came to a point at one end of the island, and across a wide channel he saw a camp of Marines. The only way to get to it was to swim across. Canavan was weak and famished, but once more he had to go navigating with side and back strokes. He was so close to exhaustion that he nearly sank, and then was nearly shot. A Marine spotted the swimmer, thought he was a Japanese, and was about to pick him off, when the lieutenant in charge stopped him. Canavan staggered to shore and collapsed in the surf. The lieutenant ran out, picked him up, and carried him to the sick bay.

It took Canavan a few weeks to recuperate at a hospital base, and then he might have been ordered back to the United States. Canavan refused to take a chance. In flagrant violation of regulations he stowed aboard a transport plane bound for Guadalcanal, determined to get back into the fighting. At Guadalcanal they asked him, "What the hell?" "Well," he drawled, "this seemed to me the place to be."

What about the Japanese cruiser that sank Canavan's boat and machine-gunned the men in the water? The enemy warship went on to Tulagi, and shelled the Americans on shore. What thereupon happened is told by Coast Guardsman Raymond Evans. "Suddenly," he relates, "a flying fortress appeared from nowhere, and everybody started to cheer. When the fort dropped a large bomb squarely on the cruiser's stern the boys went wild with enthusiasm. The bomb evidently knocked the rudder out of operation, for the cruiser went round in circles for two or three hours. After that, she managed to get under way. But the fortress came back, later reported sinking the cruiser in Sealark Channel. The Japanese paid in blood for those murders."

First among the Coast Guard heroes at Guadalcanal was Signalman Douglas A. Munro of South Cle Elum, Washington, who sacrificed his life to save a party of Marines and was decorated posthumously with the Congressional Medal of Honor. It occurred in one of those shore-line operations in which troops are taken by the boats to seize a position farther along the coast, thereby establishing a beachhead behind the enemy line. The attacking force consisted of Marines, while the boats to carry them were Coast Guard.

There were ten boats, with Signalman Munro in charge. The little fleet made a dash to the appointed place of landing, and all went well. The Marines were put ashore, where they established their beachhead and the boats returned to their starting place. There an alarming piece of news arrived. An unexpected situation had developed. The Japs in powerful force were attacking the beachhead. The defending Marines were under withering cross fire, and were in danger of being wiped out. The only way to save them was to evacuate them, the ten boats to proceed to the beachhead and take them off. Signalman Munro volunteered for the return job, and started out with his little fleet to rescue the Leathernecks from their predicament.

They got to the beachhead. Under heavy fire, as they began taking Marines aboard, a skeleton force of Leathernecks held off the Japanese, while the others embarked. That part of it was accomplished successfully, and then came the most difficult task of all: that of saving the last few Marines, the rear guard.

The Japs were swarming as these, in a fighting retreat, came down to the boats. Enemy machine gunners worked their way to a position from which they could fire on the embarking men from cover at close range. It seemed as if the Marines left on shore could never board the boat in the hail of bullets. There was nothing to cover them from the Japanese gunners. Or rather there was: a boat, Signalman Munro's boat. The Japanese were shooting across a narrow stretch of water, and the commander of the little fleet took on his own craft between the enemy machine guns and the embarking Marines in such fashion that he sheltered them from the hostile fire, his own craft taking the blast of bullets.

Two of his men fell wounded, and Signalman Munro himself sank with a mortal injury. He lay dying, but still conscious. In his last moments he asked, "Did they get off?"

He was told yes. Because of the shelter that he had given the embarking Marines, they had been taken aboard. "They're okay," he was told.

Signalman Munro smiled and died.

SERGEANT MAJOR VOOTHA, BRITISH CONSTABULARY
Silver Star Medal

Solomon Islanders, Christianized by the missionaries, were friendly toward the Americans throughout the campaign. They aided American aviators forced down their islands, and helped the Marines on Guadalcanal. The type of their loyalty is seen in the story of Sergeant Major Vootha.

THE LOYALTY OF SERGEANT MAJOR VOOTHA

THIS STORY is accompanied by an unlikely looking photograph of a hero in America's war, a black fuzzy-wuzzy of a South Sea Island tribe. He is hailed by the Marine Corps as a prodigy of valor and loyalty, and the reason points to a picturesque phase of the battle for the Solomons.

Time was when the primitive natives of the Solomons had an evil notoriety as killers and cannibals. The literature of exploration is rich with accounts of them as the most ferocious of savages. Of late years there has been a change. Missionaries have done devoted work in the Melanesian Islands off Australia

[221]

—spreading Christianity, weaning the tribes from their barbarous practices.

When, with the coming of global war, Americans and Australians clashed with the Japanese, South Sea natives gave a notable display of allegiance to their white friends. Throughout the island groups, tribes that had been cannibal not so long ago aided forced-down Allied flyers who came to their shores, and on Guadalcanal they fought in the battle against the Japanese. On that island, there was an outfit of native police organized by the Australians. They comprised a disciplined unit, and did brave, effective service. Number One among them was Sergeant Major Vootha.

He was a jungle man. He knew the equatorial forest on his native island. He could guide the Marines along obscure paths. And he could fight. The Solomon Islanders are a warlike race of ancient sanguinary tradition, and the love of battle was instinctive in Sergeant Major Vootha.

Loyalty, too, was a word the tribal warrior serving in the native police knew. Vootha was captured. The Japanese questioned him, knowing that he had an abundance of information about the American forces. When he refused to answer, the Japanese tortured him with bayonets. But he still was silent. The black tribesman whose immediate ancestors were cannibals was willing to sacrifice his life to his loyalty. The Japanese slashed him until they thought he was dead, and left him where he lay.

But Sergeant Major Vootha had life left in him, enough to escape through the Japanese lines. He returned to the Marines, and now he was full of information. He had observed things about the Japanese, their numbers, their machine-gun positions, their fortified lines. The fuzzy-wuzzy Sergeant Major transmitted valuable information to his white comrades, and was hailed as the paramount tribal warrior in the American forces on Guadalcanal.

PART NINE

AIR BATTLES OF THE SOLOMONS

LIEUTENANT COLONEL RICHARD C. MANGRUM, U.S.M.C., Seattle, Washington
Navy Cross
Distinguished Flying Cross

A Japanese destroyer, blasted by bombs. In the landing operations in the Solomons Marine Corps dive bombers, led by Lieutenant Colonel Mangrum, smashed enemy war-ships—thereby covering troops and supplies that were being put ashore.

ONE HUNDRED PERCENT MARINE

WAR FLYERS DECORATED for deeds of valor run to lieutenants largely. Most of them are young officers. Not so Lieutenant Colonel Richard C. Mangrum of the United States Marine Corps. He was thirty-six when his big moment came, and for fourteen years he had been preparing himself. He had studied gunnery and tactics, had flown in endless maneuvers, had acquired abundant experience in peacetime military flying.

Then, after all this training, came a day in August, 1942, when the Marines were seizing positions on Guadalcanal. They needed plenty of air cooperation—and got it from Army, Navy, and their own Marine Corps planes. It was altogether fair and fitting that the chief air exploit in support of the Leathernecks was accomplished by a veteran of the Marines.

Japanese warships struck as hard as they could at the landing operations, and at one critical juncture four Jap destroyers seemed about to play havoc. Marine Corps dive bombers came to the rescue, and the flight was led by Lieutenant Colonel Mangrum. The citation speaks of his "courageous leadership and utter disregard for personal safety." He was in the van of the dive-bomber attack that smashed the destroyer force. One Japanese warship was sunk. Another was blasted with everything the Americans could dish out. The third received a direct hit, the bomb bursting with devastating violence. Only one of the destroyers escaped unscathed.

The whole business was a one hundred percent Marine show—an enemy naval blow against the Leathernecks on Guadalcanal being parried by Marine dive bombers, with a veteran Lieutenant Colonel of the Marines leading them.

We have a habit of thinking of the American air forces as Army and Navy. But there is also a Marine Corps air force. The Leathernecks have a flying service of their own. The Marines are a peculiar outfit. They belong to the Navy, of course, but they are such a self-contained organization as to constitute almost a separate army. They have their own Marine Corps pride, their high tradition, their spirit of being something all by themselves. So they have their own sky fleet, which is like an individual air arm apart from Navy and Army aviation.

Marine Corps planes did heroic service in the Battle of Midway. There they operated in conjunction with the flight squadrons on the Army and the fleet. At Guadalcanal it was different. The Solomon Islands offensive was launched as a Marine Corps affair, and it remained that until the later stages when the Army took over. By the same token, the air forces based on Henderson Field were entirely Marine. The skies above Guadalcanal were a scene of endless air battles, Jap against the Leatherneck pilots.

In the early days the Henderson Field squadrons had a tough time in keeping the enemy, based on neighboring islands, from getting complete air control. Desperate odds were against them. Japanese planes raided Henderson Field constantly, trying to knock it completely out of operation. Then, as time and fighting went on, the Americans battled their way to the supremacy of the Guadalcanal skies. This was accomplished by the aerial Leathernecks, and it was a decisive factor in the winning of the final victory, the wiping out of the Japanese on Guadalcanal. A special page of honor in the history of America's first year of war is reserved for the Marine Corps air force at Henderson Field.

The Three Flying Fools of Guadalcanal—Smith, Galer and Carl. Among them, they had shot down forty-six Japanese planes, when they were decorated by Admiral Nimitz, Commander of the Pacific Fleet.

MAJOR JOHN L. SMITH, U.S.M.C., Lexington, Kentucky
Congressional Medal of Honor
Navy Cross

MAJOR ROBERT E. GALER, U.S.M.C., Seattle, Washington
Congressional Medal of Honor
Navy Cross

CAPTAIN MARION E. CARL, U.S.M.C., Woodburn, Oregon
Navy Cross
Gold Star in lieu of Second Navy Cross

Colonel Mangrum, with the two Guadalcanal rivals—Smith and Carl. They were interviewed by the press and asked about the story of how they staged their memorable Jap
destroying competition.

THE FLYING FOOLS

THE MARINE CORPS flyers on Guadalcanal were great rivals in the
business· of sending Japs crashing down out of the sky. One
squadron would run competition with another, each jealous in a
friendly way of the scores piled up by the pilots of the other, and
within a squadron the individual flyers were fiercely determined
to outdo the other, each seeking to make a better mark than
some favorite competitor. It was all very American, with a good
deal of friendly spirit, as if the shooting down of Japanese were
a sport. But it was a deadly sport, and each player of the game
knew that he might not come back from the next bout. The con-

testants saw their members decrease—familiar faces were seen no more. They would press their teeth together, and go at the game harder than ever, taking their vengeance by piling up still higher scores—each score a Japanese plane shot down, each tally a sky enemy sent to flaming doom. It was a game played by killers, with wrecked planes and dead Japanese the visible evidence of a winning performance.

Fighting Squadron 223 was an ace group, the pilots of which were savagely proud of the work of their team, the way it excelled in the deadly game, and within its own ranks there was a sharp three-cornered rivalry. In the contest were Smith, Carl, and Galer; Smith was the commander of the Fighting 223. They were the top-scoring pilots in the squadron, and the others called them "the flying fools." They went through the whole bitter air fighting for Guadalcanal and saw their squadrons diminish, one pilot gone and then another. The loss of each comrade brought a somber hour, a more bitter resolve: a resolve to get even with the cunning and bitter enemy. Smith, Carl, and Galer expressed their vengeful anger with a greater keenness of rivalry among themselves—each more determined than ever to outscore the other.

Smith was one of those chaps who did everything well. At the University of Oklahoma he was among the top men of his class. In the R.O.T.C. he was an honor student, and in his senior year became Cadet Lieutenant Colonel. After he was graduated, the Army was glad to give him a commission and he served in the field artillery. Then the Marines offered him a commission; he transferred to the soldiers of the sea, and became a flyer. He advanced steadily in rank, and, when war came to the United States, was a major.

In everything Smith excelled. Reports on him by superior officers varied from "excellent" to "outstanding." There was only one thing lacking, one qualification. Superior officers could vouch for Smith in every respect save one, "presence of mind, the ability to think and act promptly and effectively in an unexpected emergency or under great strain," as a report phrases it. In other words, in action. Smith proved himself in every circumstance except that of actual combat. In this he remained to be tested.

The test came in the Solomon Islands campaign. Major John L. Smith was in command of a Marine Corps fighter squadron, and one day his outfit got into a swirling dogfight with Zeros. How did Smith show up in the test? Individually, he shot down four Japanese in fifteen minutes.

The first two were easy, according to Smith. He got on the tail of a Zero, and this is what happened to the Japanese: "He never knew what hit him." He saw an enemy fighter attacking one of the planes of the Marine formation, banked sharply, and caught the Japanese full in his sights. That was Zero number two shot down.

Number three was really exciting, even according to the Smith standards of action and thrill. "My third Zero," he relates, "came right up under the belly of my plane, sowing bullets up and down the fuselage. I dropped the nose of my ship and came at him head on. One of his bullets hit my windshield right in front of my nose, but missed me."

The Japanese was firing plenty, but so was Smith. "My own bullets were tearing the Zero apart by this time, and huge chunks of the plane were dropping all over the place. We tore past each other less than fifteen feet apart. When I looked over my shoulder he had lost control and was spinning down."

Smith's gas was running out, and he had only a few rounds of ammunition left. He started for home, flying low. As he came over some coconut palms, a Zero, hedgehopping along the shore, came into his sights. "It wasn't even a fight," says Smith. "He crashed into the sea as the last bullet left my gun."

By the time the campaign of the Solomons was only a couple of months old, Major Smith had shot down more enemy planes than any other American war flyer. In twenty-five days he bagged sixteen Japanese, while his squadron brought down a total of eighty-three. Smith was next reported with a total of nineteen, and he kept on adding to the number. He had to keep on adding, not only to help in winning against the Japs, but also to prevail over his Marine Corps rivals. He was the pace setter for the "flying fools." On a day in September, 1942, an American plane was hit by bullets in a Solomon Islands air battle, and the pilot had to bail out. He landed in the ocean, and in his rubber boat got to an island covered with jungle. Friendly natives found him, and took him for a voyage in an outrigger canoe—returning him to the Americans on Guadalcanal. He had been missing for five days.

Upon getting back, the first thing he did was to inquire of his commanding officer: "What is Major Smith's score?"

He was told that by this time Smith had shot down sixteen Japanese planes.

"I was away five days," protested the newly rescued flyer. "Ground Smith for five, General."

That's how keen the rivalry was between Marine Corps Pilot Captain Carl and his buddy, Major John L. Smith, ace of the Marine Corps aces.

The two top men of the "flying fools," they were running neck and neck, when Carl was put to the disadvantage of being shot down and of being five days out of action. During that time Smith was up every day, bagging more Japanese. Unfair advantage, thought Carl.

The two Marine Corps flyers had many traits in common. Both were from the Pacific Northwest, Carl a native of Oregon. A born mechanic, he worked on his father's farm during summers, handling agricultural machinery, repairing tractors, tinkering with motors. Like Smith, he took a science course in college, and followed the Smith pattern of going into the Army but preferring the Marines—transferring to the soldiers of the sea as an aviation cadet.

Captain Marion E. Carl had his first taste of action against the Japanese in the Battle of Midway. He shot down one plane and damaged two others. His career crescendoed to a grand climax in the Solomon Islands. There, in a period of sixteen days, he destroyed ten Japanese planes. In partnership with another Marine flyer, he blasted an eleventh.

That was his record when he was cited for the Navy Cross, after which he kept right on going as a Japanese destroyer, soon running his count up to sixteen. Smith was still ahead of him—and Galer was not far behind. Henderson Field had its eyes on the "flying fools," and watched their scores as if they were touchdowns piled up by star football teams, traditional rivals on the gridiron. Every time there was a big air battle, the question was: How many did Smith get? What is Carl's score now? Galer added a couple to his count. The rivalry of the Flying Fools was an inspiration—to everybody but the Japanese.

Thousands of youths have taken R. O. T. C. courses, and some of the finest of American fighting men today are products of military training in land-grant colleges. Foremost among them is Major Robert Edward Galer of Guadalcanal.

He went to the University of Washington, and worked his way through—earning money for his education by operating a branch of the university bookstore. His scholastic averages were high. He was prominent in campus activities and as an athlete. He was a track man and captain of the basketball team. Bob Galer was one of Washington's great basketball players, and made an all-time record for the Pacific Coast in scoring points.

He spent four years in the N. R. O. T. C., studied naval science, became a cadet lieutenant, and took flight training at the Naval Reserve Aviation base at Seattle. Galer qualified as a carrier landing signal officer. There are not many of these officers who have the immensely responsible job of directing the landing of planes on a carrier deck.

Galer stands as a number one example of college military training, and personifies in the highest degree the qualities acquired by those tens of thousands of lads who have taken· R. O. T. C. These qualities served him well when he went to the Solomons to battle the Japs in the sky.

Leading a fighter squadron in the sky battles fought over Guadalcanal, Galer shot down eleven Jap bomber and fighter planes during a period of twenty-nine days, all of them in individual combat. Then he made it an even dozen, and kept on. His citation mentions him specifically as an altitude fighter engaging the enemy above the twenty-five-thousand-foot level. Those substratospheric altitudes are an ordeal, imposing intense hardships on the men who fly and fight wearing oxygen masks. Galer was noted for the way he stayed up there—and without taking into consideration the physical strain of extreme altitude.

Never mind, likewise, what the citation calls "seemingly unsurmountable enemy odds." Battling against odds up there where the stratosphere begins. That's the story of a star graduate of the N. R. O. T. C. who joined the Marines and the "Flying Fools."

The "Flying Fools" were an important factor in blasting the legend of the invincibility of the Japanese Zero. The Marine Corps flyers found the Zero a first-class plane. It was light, maneuverable and could climb. It was better in some ways than the planes the Leathernecks had, but it was decidedly worse in others. The Zero was not so fast at straightaway flying. With its light construction, it was not so heavily armored, and was easy to shoot down. The Marine Corps flyers brought Zeros down by the score.

During the very first days of the war the Zeros gave an impressive exhibition of their fighting power. In the tremendous Japanese sweep through the islands southeast of Asia, the Zeros led the way, and created huge havoc. Their name came to have a most formidable sound, that rather odd, negative name—Zero. People talked about them as if they couldn't be beaten.

That was quite a rebound from the previous underestimation of the Japs, a long distance away from the nonsence of saying that the Jap air force was a joke, the planes no good; the pilots incompetent, couldn't shoot, couldn't bomb, could hardly fly. Popular opinion went to the other extreme, and suddenly the Zeros became invincible.

The naval and air battles of the Coral Sea and Midway took their reputation down a notch—when carrier-based Japanese were destroyed in droves. Then the great sky fights of Guadalcanal exploded the legend completely, and showed the land-based Zero for what it was—just a very good plane.

If the Jap enemy had any particular weak point in the air, it was probably to be found in the human factor, the pilots. Not that the Japanese war flyers were bad: they were, on the contrary, very good. As an example of Japanese fatalistic courage, they did not use parachutes. For them defeat simply meant death. But that kind of morale has its drawbacks. It brings about a disproportionate loss of pilots and crews.

The most recent air battles of the southwestern Pacific have been distinguished by the great numbers of Japanese planes that our flyers have shot down, and the explanation of this, at least in part, seems to be that the Japanese pilots have deteriorated in quality. They now appear to lack practice, skill, and experience: beginners, insufficiently trained. So say American war flyers, and add the belief that the Japs lost their first line of crack pilots and had to replace them with green, poorly trained beginners. All of which leads readily to the surmise that the Japs did not train enough airmen to begin with, and consequently lacked a large enough reserve of front-line skyfighters. This looks like the weak spot of Japanese careful preparation for war: they underestimated the manpower that would be needed in the conflict of air power.

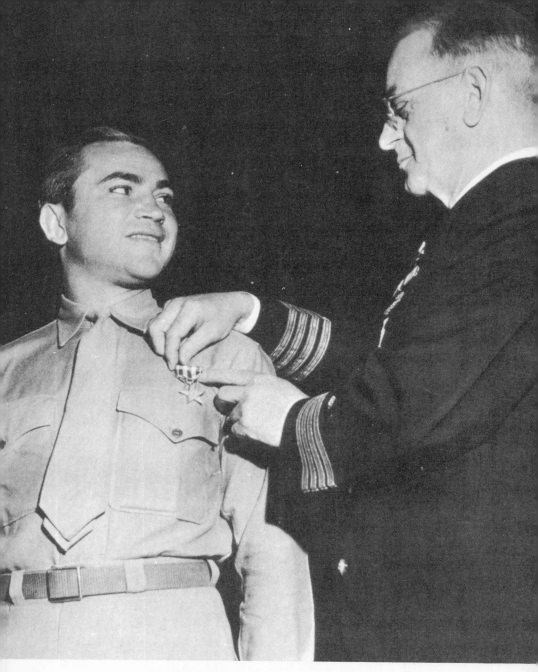

SERGEANT BARNEY ROSS, U.S.M.C., Chicago, Illinois
Silver Star Medal
Hero of Guadalcanal and former world's lightweight boxing champion, receiving the
Silver Star Medal for "conspicuous gallantry in action against the enemy" from Captain
Lester L. Pratt, U.S.N., in New York City on July 4.

BARNEY ROSS'S TOUGHEST ROUND

The citation tells the story from the viewpoint of Barney's commander, and says: "During a temporary withdrawal on the night of November 19, Private First Class Ross was missing and presumed to be a casualty. Later, it was reported that he and two comrades were alive and protecting three seriously wounded Marines left behind under heavy Japanese fire."

What happened during the time that Barney Ross was missing and presumed to be a casualty, Barney himself had better tell. He, of course, has many a story of fighting to relate—fighting in the prize ring. He had four hundred bouts with padded fists, was lightweight and welterweight champion. The Chicago lad was a tough and shifty battler, hooking, shifting, and jabbing, but all the excitement of four hundred ring bouts has turned rather dim and pale for Barney, eclipsed by that one big round on Guadalcanal. When he got back home he said: "The night I spent in that shell hole with three wounded Leathernecks and two soldiers was by all odds the toughest round I ever slugged through. I thought the bell would never sound."

It happened during a Guadalcanal crisis, when the American fighting men were pressed hard by the surging Japanese enemy. Barney Ross and five comrades were out in front. One Marine was seriously wounded. The others were trying to get him to the rear on a stretcher, when there was a Japanese rush, and they found themselves cut off from their unit. The Japs were all around them. "We dived for a pair of shell holes about ten feet apart," Barney Ross relates.

There was the situation, two shell holes, foxholes for defense. Surely it seemed as if the men in them were beyond hope, that they must certainly be mopped up by the swarming Japs. Enemy soldiers attacked them. They fought back, using rifles and hand grenades.

"In the shell hole with me," Barney tells the story, "was an Indian named Private Monak. My buddy, Private R. C. Atkins of Rome, Georgia, was in the other hole with the two other Marines." They were hit and wounded as the hours wore on.

Night came on, and in the darkness Barney Ross crawled out of his shell hole and groped around, collecting ammunition and grenades. The others were disabled, and he did the whole job himself. He collected the munitions and used them as fast as he could.

"In all," he says, "I threw twenty-one hand grenades and fired a hundred and eighty rounds of rifle ammunition. Against us the Japs were pouring in machine gun and mortar fire, but we kept them at bay."

Then he himself was wounded. In the tempest of enemy fire, no one could remain unscathed. "Some time during the night," he relates, "I got a leg and arm full of shrapnel. But, by golly, I can't tell you when it was, I was too busy to notice. I had malaria at the time, too," he adds grimly.

Day was breaking. The darkness had protected them, but now, with the rising of the sun, it seemed certain that the enemy would get them. One of the Marines called and suggested they try to get away. He proposed that they crawl out of their shell holes, to see if they could sneak toward the American lines. That seemed to be about the only thing to do.

"I crawled to him," tells the one-time prize ring champion, "and lifted him on my shoulder. Then, looking up, I beheld what looked like angels from heaven coming toward us." What was this heavenly apparition? Barney answers: "It was Captain LeBlanc, Lieutenant John Murdock, and enough of the others to make us realize that the round was over."

They were taken to the rear, where looks of surprise greeted them. Nobody expected to see them alive again. Missing, cut off by the Japanese, they had been given up for lost—casualties, dead. They looked almost dead as they were brought back badly shot up, but good hospital and medical treatment took care of that. After a while they were around again, and Barney Ross, still limping, was furloughed back home.

He was promoted, made a corporal, then a sergeant, and awarded the Silver Star Medal for conspicuous gallantry. He was acclaimed with popular ovations, the more so because he was a one-time champion with the gloves who had gained still greater glory in a larger and tougher ring.

MAJOR JOSEPH JACOB FOSS, U.S.M.C., Sioux Falls, South Dakota
Distinguished Flying Cross
Congressional Medal of Honor

The way one *Zero* took a vertical plunge after being riddled by American bullets. It is aflame, and trails a thin stream of smoke. Captain Joseph Jacob Foss established himself as the ace of all American flyers by equaling the record set by Captain Eddie Rickenbacker in the previous World War. Joe Foss wrote his name in Pacific war history as the relentless killer of the air.

KILLER JOE FOSS

THE BUSIEST JAP destroyer on Guadalcanal went to Australia for a rest. Captain Joseph Jacob Foss of the Marine Air Force had been at Henderson Field for only six weeks, which was not a long time. Many a man will go six months, or maybe six years, without a rest, but Joe Foss of Sioux Falls, South Dakota, had been most industriously occupied during his comparatively short stay. His was the relentless occupation of shooting lead into Japanese planes and pilots, ripping them apart with bullet streams like knives and sending them plunging to doom in flames. He went at the Jap with an unflagging determination, knowing no other purpose, thinking no other thought. He had the single-mindedness of an earnest worker who drives himself to the limit, and his business in hand was to make an end to Japanese. In six weeks he shot down twenty-six Japanese planes, giving him the top score among all American flyers.

But then industrious Joe Foss had lived a busy life from boyhood on. He worked on farms, ran a threshing machine, a corn sheller, and a hay bailer. He got a job as a filling station attendant, as a butcher in a market, as a laborer at a packing house. He was the janitor for his church, and when he went to college he waited on tables and washed dishes at his fraternity house. He became an aviator, a commercial pilot, and never did an airline know a harder worker, a more efficient pilot.

This was the manner of man who arrived at Guadalcanal as a war pilot, and went to work in the swirl of air fighting there. He found ample opportunity to continue his habit of doing things, never wasting a precious moment. Now industry became sheer relentlessness. Driving enterprise in peacetime vocations became ruthless energy in air fighting and sky hunting. Joe Foss combined a businesslike temperament with the killer instinct.

On October 23, 1942, one of the biggest of air battles was fought over Guadalcanal, and the clash in the sky turned out to be one of the finest American victories. Twenty Zeros and one bomber were downed, and three bombers flew away leaving trails of smoke behind them. The Marine Corps pilots lost not a plane of their own. The individual champ was Joe Foss. He was a hard-working enemy destroyer that day, as he had been, in fact, on previous days. He had already shot down six Zeros and a bomber, and in the big battle be bagged four more, bringing his score up to ten Zeros and a bomber.

Here is how Major Foss tells the story: "On October 23, when the first wave of bombers and twenty Zeros tried to attack Henderson Field, our outfit of *Grummans* got eleven Zeros and two bombers. Later we took on twenty-three Zeros in a dogfight, a regular squirrel cage that lasted twenty minutes. I got four Zeros on this hop. Those birds tried all the tricks in the bag on us—rolls, loops and what have you."

Of this lightning-fast fighting and busy-bee action by industrious Joe Foss the official record gives the following account: "He turned into a group of Zeros and nailed the first one from behind. He got on the tail of a second Jap plane and bagged it with a burst. Split seconds later, he polished off a Zero which was on the tail of a Grumman, and then shot down his fourth victim, who had made the mistake of passing him from behind."

He would have kept right on, but an oil line in his plane went bad, and he had to return to Henderson Field. There he said: "It's a good feeling to get them in your sight."

Three days later, on October 26, Foss shot down four Zeros in one hour and fifteen minutes. He was on the job incessantly, piling up an increasing total of enemies destroyed—the untiring worker on the job, the never wearying killer.

On November 12, at twenty-nine thousand feet, way up there toward the stratosphere, he had a fight with a Zero, and down it went to destruction, plunging like a stone to the sea below. And down went Foss, but in a different way. He dived to the three-thousand-foot level, a drop of twenty-six thousand feet, five miles. Why the earthward plunge? More work, another job to do, additional enemies to destroy. He spotted two rising sun torpedo bombers down there, and the sight of Japs always stirred in Joe Foss a new zest for his labor of havoc. Down he went in a roaring power dive fast enough to take the wings off the plane. The stupendous dive took him straight at the two planes. He leveled off, and shot down both of them. The first was sent plunging into the ocean before the Japanese that Foss had blasted above fell into the water. Foss, in his tremendous dive, had beaten the falling Jap in the five-mile drop—and by seconds to spare, by enough time to shoot another Jap into the sea.

Foss himself was forced down on one occasion. He flew with a squadron to attack seven enemy destroyers, and ran into enemy fighters. "One passed me," Foss relates, "and I got him. Before I could turn around, the other boys got five more."

Then Foss made a mistake which nearly cost him his life. Even the best of pilots will commit an error now and then. "I circled too near the fleet," says Foss, "and ran into two float biplanes. I overran the first one because of his slow speed. As I went by, his rear gunner got a shot at me—his bullets went through the side of the hood and out through the windshield."

Foss was forced down because of engine trouble. His motor started jerking so badly he was afraid it would rip the plane apart. Whereupon he made a landing on the sea, that spacious Coral Sea on which many an American aviator has gone drifting. He took to his rubber boat, and then the wind blew him across the water. Foss, luckily, was able to navigate to a nearby island, and there he landed.

How long did he remain marooned? Many an American flyer had waited on a South Sea atoll for days or weeks. Foss was picked up the next day, and that was largely because of his careful habits: industrious Joe. His parachute was wet, and he spread it out in the tropical sun to dry. An American scouting plane passing high above sighted that vivid spot on the ground: the spreading white silk of a parachute stretched out.

These incidents are typical of the six weeks that Joe Foss spent on Guadalcanal, after which he was sent over to Australia for what can surely be described as a "well-earned rest." But he was too energetic to rest for long, and soon was busy again shooting down Japs.

That was indicated in a telegram which was given front-page publicity. It was from Captain Eddie Rickenbacker, American flying ace in the first World War, and was addressed to Captain Joseph Jacob Foss in the Solomon Islands.

The telegram read: "Just heard that you have shot down your twenty-sixth enemy airplane, which equals my record of victories in World War Number One. I hasten to offer my heartiest congratulations, with the hope that you will double it."

Months after the Battle of Guadalcanal was over, Joe Foss went to Washington, to the White House, where he received the Congressional Medal of Honor from President Roosevelt. The tall and singularly handsome flyer was feted and acclaimed, interviewed and photographed. He took it with more confusion than he had ever displayed in the face of Zeros in the sky.

While the ace of the Southwest Pacific was in the United States, the atrocious news broke that the Japanese had executed some of the Doolittle flyers. Instantly one single ambition flashed in every American war pilot, the hot and wrathful desire to bomb Tokyo again and again and again. No one expressed this better than Joe Foss, in his homespun South Dakota way. He told the newspapermen: "Everyone's ambition is to get to Tokyo, and I'd like to get there and sort of talk over those executions. It's kind of hard to say how you feel about a thing like that," he added, "but I'd sure like to talk it over out there." Talk it over with bombs—in that kind of conversation in which reticent and modest Joe Foss could be loud and eloquent.

LIEUTENANT HAROLD H. LARSEN, U.S.N., Birmingham, Alabama
Navy Cross
Distinguished Flying Cross
Lieutenant Larsen after surviving twenty-seven attacks on Nipponese ships and bases
returns home. Here he is explaining to his wife that the Japs were not responsible for
his hand injury, which was caused on the return trip home.

A Navy torpedo plane has just discharged its tin fish, which is seen hitting toward the water. The torpedo with its propellers whirling, trails a wake of carbon dioxide. This gas, compressed, gives its motor power. Most famous of all was Torpedo Squadron 8, which sacrificed itself to victory at Midway. Reconstituted and sent to the Solomons, Torpedo 8 was placed under the command of Swede Larsen, who established an in_dividual record as the man who made more successful torpedo runs than any other.

TORPEDO ACE

ONE EVENING RECENTLY there were some guests in the N.B.C. studio at my daily news broadcast. One was a young naval officer who kept unobtrusively in the background. He had come with some-body else, and was introduced as Lieutenant Larsen. When the program was over, he left with a quiet good-by. Then, after he was gone, I was told: "That was Swede Larsen, Commander of Torpedo Squadron 8."

I said, "Holy smoke!"

Torpedo Squadron 8, that outfit of Navy torpedo planes which fought to death and immortality at the Battle of Midway!

After Midway, Torpedo Squadron 8 was reconstituted and went on to new heights of heroism in the battles of the Solomons. The superb honor of being its commander was given to Lieutenant Harold Larsen of Omaha—Swede Larsen.

During four months in the Solomons, he led Torpedo Squadron 8 in twenty-seven attacks, during which his planes hit every type of Japanese warship from battleship to destroyer. Swede Larsen, himself, is on record as the flyer who, to date, has made more successful torpedo runs against enemy ships than any other man alive.

He earned a decoration. The Marines were landing on Guadalcanal. They needed air cover, and Swede Larsen and Torpedo 8 were ordered to support the invasion force. They discarded their tin fish, took bomb loads aboard, and assailed the enemy on land, blasting Jap positions and concentrations.

On August 24 Torpedo 8 did its normal task—with torpedoes. Larsen led his planes against a Japanese task force. In the middle of the task force, in the vortex of the storm of antiaircraft fire and whirling Zeros, was a Japanese cruiser. It was the toughest kind of target, but they reached it, and scored a direct hit with a torpedo.

On November 7 the target was a Japanese force of one light cruiser and ten destroyers. Larsen's planes operated in conjunction with fighters and dive bombers and their contribution was a torpedo hit on the cruiser.

To what does the commander of Torpedo 8 attribute his success? Larsen names his mechanic—James Clyde Hammond, Aviation Chief Machinist's Mate. "My husband," writes Mrs. H. H. Larsen, "gives him great credit for his bravery and skill in preparing planes at Guadalcanal under fire at Henderson Field."

The place to talk about Swede Larsen is Birmingham, his Alabama home town. But Birmingham has still another favorite hero: Noel Gayler of the *Lexington*. Larsen and Gayler are both from Birmingham. In addition to the home-town picture, there's a family angle. Swede Larsen and Noel Gayler are cousins by marriage.

PART TEN

THE NAVAL EPIC OF THE SOUTHWEST PACIFIC

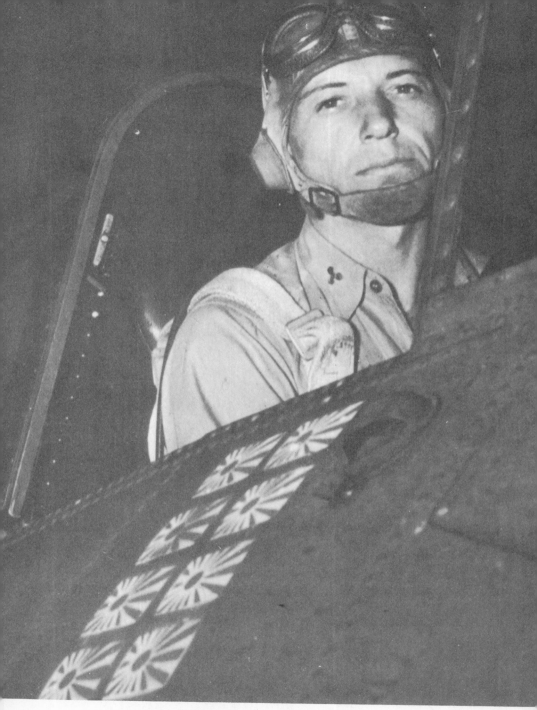

MACHINIST DONALD E. RUNYON, U.S.N., La Jolla, California
Distinguished Flying Cross

A Japanese heavy bomber found adrift minus its tail shows the way many a Japanese plane has met an end after being shot down by American planes. The Jap pilot may be seen on the right wing to the right of the open cockpit.

FIGHTING SIX

THIS IS THE story of a day with Fighting Six. On August 24 that carrier-based group of Wildcat fighters shot down twenty-seven Japanese planes in one battle. Fighting Six lost four—two pilots saved. The top scorer was Pilot Machinist Donald E. Runyon of Ellisville, Mississippi. But first let us see what Don Runyon's comrades did.

Fighting Six took off to protect the warships against hostile air attack, and Ensign Barns was first to score a victory. He caught a Japanese scout flying in advance of bombers, and shot it down.

Next Ensign Register hit a Zero so hard the pilot was seen to jump without a parachute. Register swung around, caught another enemy in his sights, and down the Japanese went in flames.

Lieutenant Vorse gave a Zero a burst. Flames shot out of the cockpit. The fire died down, but the Zero was plunging, and it flamed anew as it hit the water.

Machinist Sumrall destroyed a Zero, while Ensign Brooks fired into a dive bomber from the side. The dive bomber kept on diving —into the sea. Ensign March took a long shot at a torpedo plane. He fired a mere tentative burst, hardly expecting to score a hit at so great a range, but the Zero plunged into the water.

Radio Electrician Rhodes and Aviation Pilot Mankin got a dive bomber each. Mankin went after another. The Japanese tried so hard to get away that he flew into the water. Mankin did not list this one as "shot down." The Japanese downed himself.

One dive bomber was getting through to the American ships. Lieutenant Bower shot it down, and then got mixed up with a Zero. He scored a hit, but the Zero dived away and escaped him. Ensign Halford caught it: good-bye Zero.

One Japanese was a first-class acrobat. Six Wildcats of Fighting Six went after him but he stunted his way out. Another tried stunting with Lieutenant Gay. But Gay outstunted him, and got in his burst as the enemy was doing a cartwheel.

Ensign Shoemaker took after a diving dive bomber. He was too fast, and ran past it, but that took him on to the tail of another farther down. One more victory was scored when a Zero got on the tail of a Wildcat; Ensign Lindsey came to the rescue, and knocked it out.

Ensign Disque shot down one Zero and then another, but a third Zero riddled Disque's plane. The Ensign got back to the carrier, but his plane was counted a total loss when they examined it. The pilot was only slightly wounded. Ensign Johnson, while downing a Jap, had the left aileron of his plane shot away, the propeller was hit by a bullet and the wings were riddled. But Johnson got back.

Ensign Dibb set a dive bomber afire at fourteen thousand feet, at ten thousand feet took a shot at a Zero, and then swung off to shoot down a dive bomber. Gunner Brewer was operating at a low altitude. He bagged a dive bomber at four thousand feet, dived down to the surface of the water and found a Jap close in front of him and coming right at him. He riddled it, and it plunged, certain collision avoided. Still near the surface of the sea, Brewer shot down a Zero that passed him.

With exploits like these marked to the credit of others of Fighting Six, what about the champion of the day? Machinist Runyon was somewhat of a sun worshipper. He placed his faith in the shining god of day. At eighteen thousand feet he came out of the sun to attack a dive bomber, which blew up when hit. Runyon swung back up into the sun, and came out of it again to get another dive bomber. A sunny disposition had Runyon! He was returning up into the sunbeams, when a Zero swung in front of him. Down went the Zero, exploding. Runyon was still trying to get up into the sun, when he saw a chance to zoom up under a dive bomber. That ended another Jap.

Don't count this next one. Runyon got in a burst of fire, and the Zero plunged down to the sea, trailing smoke. It leveled off at the water, and may have got away. Probably not; but that Japanese doesn't count on Runyon's record. The sun worshipper is credited with having shot down only four in that one fight.

ADMIRAL WILLIAM F. HALSEY, JR., U.S.N., Washington, D. C.
Distinguished Service Medal

Pacific fleet Commander Admiral Nimitz talks over matters of naval strategy with "Give 'em Halsey." As Commander of naval operations in the Solomons, Admiral Halsey directed the sea victories that assured the wiping out of the Japanese on Guadalcanal.

GIVE 'EM HALSEY

THE KEY to the American victory in the six months of fighting on Guadalcanal Island was provided by the Navy. The reason the Marines and then regular army troops were able to wipe out the Japs on land was because the Navy defeated the enemy at sea. Our lines of communication were kept open. Those of the Japanese were cut. We were able to supply and reinforce. They were not. This was the result of a series of naval engagements in the area of the Solomons, engagements in which the Japanese fleet made determined attempts to break through to Guadalcanal. At times they did succeed in landing some supplies and troops, but were seldom able to do more than sneak a few crates and troops in at night.

In speaking of the sea fights revolving around Guadalcanal, we commonly use the general term "The Solomons." But the Navy lists five separate battle names:

The Battle of Savo Island was a bad one for us, when a surprise Japanese naval attack sank three American cruisers and one Australian cruiser.

The Battle of the Eastern Solomons, when a Japanese fleet tried to get to Guadalcanal and sustained heavy damage to a number of vessels, including a battleship.

The Battle of Cape Esperance in which our ships smashed a Jap task force and sank two heavy cruisers, one light cruiser, and three destroyers. We lost one destroyer. This was the engagement in which the American cruiser *Boise* was the hero ship.

The Battle of Santa Cruz Islands, in which the enemy sustained the loss of two destroyers and heavy damage to carriers, battleships and lighter vessels. We lost an aircraft carrier, the *Hornet*.

The Battle of Guadalcanal which was the climax, a crushing American victory. This was the biggest fight of the entire war of the Pacific, and it was decisive. With the Japanese making their greatest attempt to drive to Guadalcanal and land large forces, the fleet saved the island. The enemy lost one battleship sunk, and another powerful Japanese vessel that may have been a battleship or a cruiser was sent to the bottom. Eight enemy cruisers were sunk, six destroyers, and twelve transports. Two Japanese battleships, one destroyer, and six cruisers damaged. We lost two light cruisers and seven destroyers—a heavy cruiser damaged. The epic of the engagement was the fight put up by the American flagship, the cruiser *San Francisco*.

The number one figure in the successful sea campaign was a sturdy, square-cut officer of whom you could say at a glance: "there's a seafaring man." Admiral Bill Halsey had all the look and manner of a salt-bitten sailor, bushy-browed face, pugnacious jaw, weather-wise eyes, rakish air, and swagger gait, sea legs accustomed to a deck. His outward semblance was an accurate expression of his inner personality: bold decision, daring tactics, swift striking.

These were qualities that Bill Halsey had previously displayed in the heat of action off the Gilbert and Marshall Islands. He had commanded the American task force that had raided those Japanese strongholds early in the war, and his handling of the attacking ships had drawn this comment from the Commander in Chief of the Pacific fleet, Admiral Nimitz: "Aggressive, audacious, yes, but not reckless."

In the Gilbert and Marshall raid the key to the strategy was a quadrangle of fortified enemy islands, four sea and air bases making the square. Halsey's flagship was an aircraft carrier. This he took to the middle of the quadrangle, and sent out all his planes to bomb. They flew from a central position to strike at all sides. Favorable for offense, but what about the defensive phase of the situation? There is nothing so helpless as a carrier without planes to protect it, and there was Halsey's flat-top in a square of enemy air bases, surrounded by air bases. You might think a commander mad to put his ship in that position. You might have expected Japanese planes to swarm from their four angles and sink the carrier so completely lacking in air protection.

Halsey knew what he was doing. His cruisers had previously shelled the Japanese island positions in a surprise bombardment, and his skill lay in the fact that he had accurately gauged the effect of the gunfire. In cold-blooded calculation he reckoned that the naval bombardment had put the Japanese air bases sufficiently out of commission to make things reasonably safe for his carrier.

He was right. Only a handful of Japanese planes took off, and these the carrier repelled with antiaircraft fire, while its planes were absent, giving the Japanese hell with bombs.

First in the Gilbert and Marshall Islands and then in the Solomons, Halsey acted on the saying attributed to him on the day of Pearl Harbor. He remarked grimly that, by the time we were through, "the Japanese language would be spoken only in hell." Halsey is salty of speech as well as looks, and his sailors refer to him as "Give 'Em Halsey."

COMMODORE EDWARD J. MORAN, U.S.N., San Francisco, California
Navy Cross

The United States light cruiser *Boise*, hero ship of sea battle off the Solomon Islands. Spick-and-span in the picture, the *Boise* was very badly damaged in a clash with the Japanese. It sank a stream of enemy vessels and then got safely back to an American base.

MORAN OF THE *BOISE*

COMMODORE EDWARD JOSEPH MORAN of Chicago once supervised an election in Nicaragua, and a Nicaraguan election could be something on the order of a pitched battle. The legal government, which was recognized by the United States, appointed the United States naval officer to run its nationwide ballot-box contest. Moran of Chicago handled the Central American election so well that he was awarded a Nicaraguan decoration. Moran was versatile, and after having distinguished himself in the matter of votes and candidates, he went on to win glory with guns and broadsides in naval battle.

[259]

It happened in the Solomons: the Battle of Cape Esperance. That was the fight in which the cruiser *Boise* was the hero ship, and Moran commanded the *Boise*. A powerful enemy naval force moved in to land reinforcements for the Japanese on Guadalcanal, a sneak landing at night. American warships raced to intercept the enemy squadron. The *Boise* was in the forefront. Suddenly hostile warships were spotted at close range in the darkness—six of them. The *Boise* ran smack into two heavy cruisers, a light cruiser, and three destroyers. The two larger enemy ships had eight-inch cannons to the six-inchers of the *Boise*. Did it try to get out of the desperate corner? Did it try to evade the huge enemy force? Not at all.

"Pick a big one," said Moran, then Captain, giving the order for battle.

In the face of outnumbering odds of six ships to one ship, and of eight-inch guns to his six-inch guns, he opened fire on a heavy Japanese cruiser.

His first short-range salvo, fired at an indistinct silhouette spied in the darkness, hit the Japanese and set a fire amidships. The blaze lit up the target nicely, and the *Boise* fired with everything she had for four minutes. The enemy heavy cruiser plunged, going down by the bows.

While polishing off the larger adversary, the *Boise* meanwhile was being attacked by a Japanese destroyer. The secondary batteries of the American cruiser disposed of that enemy. The destroyer disappeared below the surface.

Slugging in close in a nocturnal orgy of shellfire, the *Boise* engaged and sank all six of the Japanese warships. It was an almost incredible feat of battle, which earned for the *Boise* the proud name, One Ship Fleet.

But it was not all giving. There was plenty of taking. Through the fight the *Boise* was in an enemy cross fire. She fired a thousand rounds in twenty-seven minutes of battle and was hit by eleven salvos. An eight-inch shell smashed a hole nine feet below her water line. A magazine exploded, and flames spurted above the mast. A hundred and seven of her crew were killed. The blazing and erupting *Boise* staggered across the water and was lost to the view of the other American ships. They thought she was lost.

But Captain Moran wasn't giving up the ship so easily. He had his crew flood the flaming magazine. The *Boise* was so badly ablaze that they had to fight the fire from stem to stern. Bulkheads had been sprung by the shock of exploding shells. These were tightened. They plugged the gaping shell hole nine feet below the water line—stuffed it with mattresses, bedding.

Two hours after the *Boise* had disappeared from the view of the other American ships, she reappeared to join the column, limping, down by the head, but ready to go on fighting.

No sight could have been more heartening to the men of the other warships than this reappearance of the comrade cruiser that they had given up for lost. Instead of lying on the bottom of the sea or drifting somewhere as a hulk only fit to be sunk as a menace to navigation, lo, and behold, there was the *Boise* steaming into the line of ships, ready to take her accustomed place. True, she was badly battered, but it was a miracle that she was there at all. That was the cheering news which flashed among the ships of the fleet—and then around the world.

Later the crippled *Boise* was able to steam halfway round the world to the United States—to the Philadelphia Navy Yard for repairs. The One Ship Fleet received a hero's welcome. Admiral King, our naval Commander in Chief, went aboard and gave the Navy's congratulations to Captain Moran and his crew. The *Boise* was repaired, and then in due time put out to sea to fight again.

LIEUTENANT COMMANDER WILLIAM G. WIDHELM, U.S.N., Humphrey, Nebraska
Navy Cross

A thriller of battles is pictured, as Japanese torpedo planes and dive bombers attack the *Hornet*. As two torpedo planes fly low, a stick of air bombs narrowly misses the *Hornet*. A Japanese dive bomber plunges, and a moment later crashes into the carrier, blowing up as it hits the signal bridge. The *Hornet* was sunk in the Battle of the Santa Cruz Islands. But before it went to the warrior's end, the glorious flat-top revenged itself in advance by sinking Japanese warships. Lieutenant Commander Widhelm led his "Bombing Fools" against the biggest aircraft carrier in the world.

THE LAST STING OF THE *HORNET*

BEFORE THE *Hornet* was sunk in the Battle of the Santa Cruz Islands the carrier had accomplished the following, which the official naval report calls "minimum results": At least one torpedo hit on a carrier. Two one-thousand-pound and one five-hundred-pound bomb hits and two one-thousand-pound near misses on battleships. One one-thousand-pound hit on a heavy cruiser, later seen sinking, survivors abandoning ship. Six one-thousand-pound bomb hits on another cruiser. Two five-hundred-pound bomb hits on destroyers. One destroyer strafed by fighters. Four ten-thousand-ton transports, with a capacity of approximately five thousand men each, sunk. Seven one-thousand-pound bomb hits on a carrier larger than any American carrier, the destruction of which monster flat-top was the last blow the *Hornet* struck: the last sting.

The *Hornet's* torpedo planes were a great outfit. They shot their tin fish with deadly aim, and varied this by dropping depth bombs and, if you think that the letting go of a depth charge does not require a keen aim, consider the following: On one breathless occasion a Japanese submarine nearly got the *Hornet*. The enemy undersea craft stole in close, maneuvered into firing position, and sent a torpedo speeding directly at the hull of the *Hornet*, a certain hit apparently. A plane from the *Hornet* happened to be flying low in the vicinity, and the pilot saw the streaking torpedo. He swerved over that way, and took aim with a depth bomb that he was carrying. He discharged the ponderous charge of high explosive with such accuracy that the explosion changed the course of the torpedo. The fish turned off in another direction, missing the carrier completely.

The *Hornet's* dive bombers were called "the Bombing Fools." That's how the fleet out in the Solomon Islands paid tribute to the air squadron led by Lieutenant Commander William J. Widhelm of Humphrey, Nebraska. At Midway the Bombing Fools smashed a battleship, which they listed as sunk. Widhelm personally scored thousand-pound bomb hits on two cruisers of the *Nogami* and *Mikuma* classes. These two were sunk. Then the *Hornet* went out to the Solomons, and there the Bombing Fools continued their folly: foolish like a cross between a fox and a tiger. They raided Japanese positions and shot down Jap planes, and then came the Battle of Santa Cruz Islands.

Widhelm's Bombing Fools were given the brief order: "Get the carrier." It was of the *Zuikaku* class, a flat-top which the pilots later described as being bigger than either the *Lexington* or *Saratoga*, America's biggest. The Japanese plane-launching giant was of the largest type extant. Carriers are always the number one targets for the assaulting planes, and this was the number one carrier.

The Bombing Fools numbered fifteen. They had to fly for half an hour and for a distance of seventy-five miles before they got to the *Zuikaku*. During that time and for that distance they traveled a road of a thousand perils, *Zeros* all the way, *Zeros* attacking every minute and every mile. The Bombing Fools shot down fifteen, of which two were blasted to oblivion by Widhelm himself. One tried to ram him, the Japanese pilot speeding straight on for a collision, only to be shattered by bullets and sent for an abrupt plunge when only a few feet and a fraction of a second intervened.

They lost two, two of their own shot down during the long run and the attack. Two others were damaged and had to take refuge in the clouds. Fifteen Bombing Fools to begin with, four out of action, eleven left for the assault on the monster flat-top.

Widhelm himself was one of the two shot down. Jap bullets ripped his plane as he approached the *Zuikaku*, and down he came for a landing on the sea, his plane sinking, he and his gunner, Aviation Radioman George D. Stokeley of Newport, Tennessee, getting out safely. They launched their rubber boat, clambered aboard, and had ringside seats for the destruction of the *Zuikaku*. They were so near they could spot every bomb that fell and burst. Widhelm saw his Bombing Fools put into practice the maneuvers he had taught them—the disciplined peel-off and dive and the precise laying of the thousand pounders. He saw seven one-thousand-pounds strike the deck of the carrier with shattering blasts. The huge flat-top burst into spouting flames. The entire length of the sea giant became an inferno, swept by fire, erupting with explosions.

In their rubber boat ringside seats Widhelm and Stokeley could cheer as if each hit were a touchdown scored in a football game. But all was not so quiet for the two men in the boat. Japanese warships appeared, steaming past from over the horizon, and they headed straight for Widhelm and Stokeley—apparently about to run over them, which would have been a strange end for two American airmen. In any case, the enemy might shoot them, the ships were passing that close. Japs on the decks could readily have seen and machine-gunned them.

Widhelm and Stokeley flopped out of their boat, and hid

under it, clinging to it and keeping under and out of sight as much as possible. There concealed, all they had to worry about was sharks. The waters of the Solomons abound in the killer fish, as they well knew. Sharks were a prevalent nightmare of the Americans out there. Widhelm and Stokeley, dangling in the water under the boat, felt themselves to be tempting morsels for huge, gaping jaws filled with spikelike teeth. They kicked, thrashed their legs, and made as much commotion in the water as they could to frighten the sharks. Meanwhile the Jap warships were passing close by, tossing their rubber boat like a cockleshell.

The enemy ships went speeding toward the horizon, and Widhelm and Stokeley climbed back into their rubber boat. All they had to do now was drift, hoping to be picked up or be blown by the wind to an island. They were afloat for three days. Out of their parachutes they rigged a sail and a sea anchor—resourceful mariners those two. They were navigating toward an island when a Navy patrol plane spotted them and picked them up, returning them to the Bombing Fools for further air assaults against the enemy.

The *Hornet* herself was assailed, and went down to a grave at the bottom of the Pacific. She fought it out to the last, blasted by bombs, on fire and shaken by explosions in her vitals. She was the carrier that had taken the Doolittle flyers to the bombing of Tokyo, and the Japanese promptly did some tall bragging. They claimed that they had gone after the *Hornet* out of vengeance for that stroke against their supposedly invulnerable country. From the day of the Tokyo bombing they had hunted for the *Hornet*, and finally had got her—so they said.

We may smile at this, and wonder whether they would not have flown with equal determination against any other American carrier in the battle. Do they, in a naval action, assault ships because of particular grudges? Or do they fight against any hostile craft in front of them? The tale of a feud against the *Hornet* sounds like the usual Japanese propaganda—the wily enemy trying to use a success in a naval battle as a way to save face. They lost plenty of face when Japan was bombed, and at a late date sought to restore their physiognomy with a pretense of successful vendetta.

A theme of vengeance practiced on our side is found in the subsequent careers of the airmen of the *Hornet*, who after destruction of their carrier, went on flying against the Japs. Steeled with a resolution to avenge the *Hornet*, they went to new tasks of war—dive bombing enemy ships and waging air battles against enemy fighting planes. During the months that have followed that sea and air battle in the Solomons, when the carrier was sunk, the sky fighters of the *Hornet* have exacted ample vengeance for the loss of their ship.

REAR ADMIRAL DANIEL J. CALLAGHAN, U.S.N. (Deceased), Oakland, California
Congressional Medal of Honor

COMMANDER BRUCE McCANDLESS, U.S.N., Long Beach, California
Congressional Medal of Honor

COMMANDER HERBERT E. SCHONLAND, U.S.N., New London, Connecticut
Congressional Medal of Honor

The *San Francisco* returns home, and the gallant cruiser shows the signs of battle. The *San Francisco* was a glory ship in the great naval battle of Guadalcanal, when the Japs were decisively defeated. Aboard the cruiser Admiral Callaghan was killed, as was the *San Francisco's* skipper, Captain Cassin Young. The command devolved on Lieutenant Commander Schonland, who passed the honor on to his junior, Lieutenant Commander Mc-Candless—giving him the distinction of commanding the *San Francisco* through the remainder of the battle.

THE *SAN FRANCISCO*

THE NAVAL battle of Guadalcanal was made memorable by the gallantry of admirals. Two lost their lives while commanding their ships in daring maneuvers. Each conceived of bold tactics to which he sacrificed himself. Both Admiral Daniel J. Callaghan and Admiral Norman Scott were close personal friends of President Roosevelt, who conferred posthumous decorations on them. Admiral Callaghan had been the President's aide.

The story of the Battle of Guadalcanal is dominated by the names of Callaghan and the *San Francisco*. Aboard that hero cruiser, his flagship, the Admiral led his naval column in a maneuver that ranks as a classic of bold surprise. The Japanese, in their interminable attempts to land reinforcements on Guadalcanal, came in with their warships in three columns. In this arrangement of the enemy force Admiral Callaghan saw his chance to strike with the completely unexpected. He took his line of ships between two of the enemy columns. He had nothing heavier than cruisers. They had battleships. Rash, apparently. But it worked, although the Admiral gave his life to prove it.

The line of American cruisers steaming through the corridor between the two enemy lines ran a gauntlet of enemy cross fire. They were shot at from both sides, and the Jap battleships outgunned the cruisers tremendously. The Americans had to take heavy punishment, but the surprise of the exploit was such that the Japs lost their advantage. They were so confused that they fired at their own ships. Blundering in the cross fire that they hurled at the Americans, they cannonaded each other. Thus a signal American victory was won in the biggest sea fight of the Solomons. The enemy sustained the heaviest losses, our cruisers accomplishing the feat of sinking a battleship.

Admiral Callaghan's flagship led the dash between the two Japanese columns. The *San Francisco* got in the first blows, and took the first blows. The Admiral gave a memorable order: "Go after the big ones." This the *San Francisco* did, engaging a Japanese battleship of the *Kongo* class. No cruiser, with its lighter guns, can match the ponderous ordnance of a battleship—or so the theory ran.

The *San Francisco* engaged the *Kongo* class giant and inflicted damage that crippled it. The battleship was finished off later by other American vessels. But in the close-range slugging the *San Francisco* took savage punishment; she was hit by repeated salvos from enemy ships on both sides and was blasted frightfully by the giant shells from the battleship.

In the inferno of steel and fire was played a memorable human drama. A shell hit the cruiser's bridge, where the commanding officers were. The blast wrecked the bridge and killed the commanding officers. Admiral Callaghan perished, and so did the Captain of the *San Francisco*—Captain Cassin Young.

With them was a young Lieutenant Commander, Bruce McCandless. He was tossed around by the explosion, injured, knocked unconscious. When he came to, he found the bridge a gory shambles of wreckage and shattered bodies, a ghastly scene of twisted steel and men blown to pieces. Then McCandless found all that was left of the Admiral and the Captain. Both had perished in the explosion. Other officers had been killed or desperately wounded, and because of the casualties the young Lieutenant Commander found himself the senior officer on the bridge. That put him in command of the flagship, which in turn directed the movements of the other vessels in the American column. Later, when the news broke, Americans were to thrill to the story of how the thirty-one-year-old Lieutenant Commander led the squadron through the remainder of the triumphant battle.

Although left the senior officer on the bridge, McCandless was not next in rank to the Admiral and the Captain among the officers on the ship. Because of seniority rules and the casualties of battle, top rank was now held by another Lieutenant Commander—Herbert Emery Schonland, damage officer of the *San Francisco*. Navy regulations designated him to succeed to the command of the flagship. At the time Admiral Callaghan and Captain Young were killed he was far below decks, doing his job as damage control officer, and there was much to do. It would have been routine for him to go up to the bridge and assume command of the *San Francisco*, replacing McCandless.

There you have a situation with a vivid human angle. What Lieutenant Commander would not have jumped at the chance to command a cruiser in action, the flagship, and thereby lead the squadron in battle? Nearly any junior officr would give his right arm for the chance, the opportunity for fame. Headlines would blazon the dramatic event. The limelight that would flash! Lucky officer! So what did Schonland do?

Below decks he ascertained that McCandless was doing all right on the bridge. Whereupon he telephoned the word: "Tell McCandless to take command. I'm too busy fighting fire."

Busy indeed he was, up to his waist in water, directing the battle against the blaze. The battered *San Francisco* was imperiled by flooded compartments and badly on fire. To cope with that was Schonland's job, and with him a job came first. He renounced the distinction of commanding the cruiser and a column of warships in battle. Below decks, and battling fire and water, he stayed on the job that enabled the *San Francisco* to continue fighting, doing the damage control work that kept the ship from sinking or blowing up.

On the bridge, McCandless, commanding cruiser and squadron, completed the glorious maneuver devised by the Admiral, and scrupulously obeyed the Admiral's order, "Go after the big ones," which strategy completed the culminating American victory in the naval campaign of the Solomons.

Schonland and McCandless received the same decoration from President Roosevelt. The President emphasized the unselfishness of Schonland, who, without egotism, had turned over to another officer so great a distinction.

The naval battle of Guadalcanal was not only the climax of the sea fighting in the Solomons area but it had an important bearing on the strategy of warfare at sea. The battles of the Coral Sea and Midway had suddenly brought about startling new innovations in sea warfare—fleets battling it out with their planes, hostile sea forces fighting major engagements without the rival warships ever coming in sight of each other. People started to say that the day of the tremendous gun duels had gone, and that hereafter warfare on the ocean would be a matter of planes against ships, with carriers playing the dominant role. There was talk that battleships were obsolete, their ponderous broadsides as much a thing of the past as the flights of arrows at Cressy.

That was the state of opinion when the battles of the Solomons began. But in the engagements on the ocean around Guadalcanal the exclusive conflict of planes against ships failed to materialize. Instead there was a series of clashes between warships, each pounding the other with guns, slugging it out with shellfire. In a slugging duel there's nothing like a battleship and the armored giants came back into their own.

There was a decided trend back to the tried and true naval

warfare—warships versus warships, guns against guns—and this was seen most vividly in the Battle of Guadalcanal. That culminating American victory was old-fashioned in the sense that the conflict was a head-on meeting of warships, with gunnery as the striking power. It was followed by a considerable revision of expressed opinion. Battleships were spoken of again with respect, and the carrier and its planes were no longer considered to be the exclusive striking arm.

REAR ADMIRAL NORMAN SCOTT, U.S.N. (Deceased), Washington, D. C.
Congressional Medal of Honor

U.S.S. Atlanta, light cruiser

A FIGHTER ADMIRAL

REAR ADMIRAL NORMAN SCOTT distinguished himself in both World Wars. In the previous conflict he was Executive Officer on the destroyer *Jacob Jones*, which was torpedoed by a German submarine, December 6, 1917. The destroyer sank rapidly, and saving the lives of members of the crew was the major task. In this Executive Officer Norman Scott took a leading part. His job was to get lifebelts and splinter nets from the bridge into the water. This he did with a magnificent display of coolness, energy, and seamanship. He helped imperiled men. He encouraged them on to safety. The saving of many lives was marked to his credit.

During the twenty-four years between wars this extremely competent officer went through the routine naval duty and promotion. He became a Rear Admiral, and when the Japanese struck he was in line for an important command. He was given assignments of vital consequence in the Southwestern Pacific and played his part in two mighty clashes with the Japanese.

One was the Battle of Cape Esperance, when a powerful Japanese naval squadron tried to storm its way to Guadalcanal and land reinforcements there. Admiral Scott commanded the American task force that intercepted the enemy. A violent engagement ensued, in which the Admiral's bold and skilful tactics drove off the enemy with the loss of eight ships.

A month later, in the Battle of Guadalcanal, he was in the thick of the desperate close-range fighting, as the Japs once again tried to put reinforcements ashore on Guadalcanal. The Admiral's own flagship, the *Atlanta*, plunged into the attack against desperate odds, blasting the enemy with repeated salvos. Facing tremendously superior fire power, the *Atlanta* was hit heavily, and in the explosions that ensued the Admiral was killed.

Months later, at the City of Atlanta, Georgia, a new cruiser was launched to take the place of the *Atlanta* that had come to a warrior's end in the Battle of Cape Esperance. Secretary of the Navy Frank Knox was the principal speaker at the ceremony. "From the beginning," he said, "the *Atlanta* was a marked ship. She represented a new class which we believe was the most powerful of its type ever built. Apparently the enemy agreed with us, for they knew they would have to gang up on her.

"In that fatal battle," Secretary Knox went on, "the *U.S.S. Atlanta* faced many times her own weight and many times her own guns. She took everything the Japs could find in their magazines. Yes, she took everything they had—and in return she sent two Jap ships to the bottom and helped to sink others before the action ended.

"And at dawn, after that night battle, the entire Jap force was either on the bottom or on the run. But the *Atlanta* was still there, wounded and out of action, but her flag was still flying. For all their ganging up, the Japs did not sink her. The *U.S.S. Atlanta*, God bless her memory, was given a burial with honor at the hands of her gallant commander, Captain Samuel P. Jenkins, and her gallant men.

"It is to our great national loss," the Secretary concluded, "that some of her men were not to survive their ship's last action. One of these was Rear Admiral Norman Scott, finest product of the American naval school of seamanship and strategy."

LIEUTENANT COMMANDER W. E. HANK, U.S.N., (Deceased), Norfolk, Virginia
Navy Cross

An oceanic battle scene, the sky mottled with antiaircraft fire. A Japanese plane is hit by a shell from a warship off the Solomons. The spectacle is one that was witnessed constantly by American sailors in the battles of the Southwest Pacific.

DESTROYER VERSUS BATTLESHIP

THERE WAS something of the drama of the Blue and the Gray in the association of the ship and her commander, the destroyer *Laffey* and Lieutenant Commander William Edwin Hank.

The *Laffey* represented the Blue. She was named after an Irish-American sailor who distinguished himself fighting for the Union in the War Between the States. He was a member of a ship's crew that at Yazoo City went ashore and fought against Confederate attack. Battling with a cannon in the street, Seaman Laffey comported himself so valorously that sixty years later a United States destroyer was named after him.

Lieutenant Commander William Edwin Hank was from down in Dixieland, where the uniform at that time was gray. He was a native of Norfolk, Virginia, and down there the traditions were of Lee and Stonewall Jackson.

A Southerner in command of a destroyer named after a Yankee sailor of the Civil War, that combination was glorious in the Battle of Guadalcanal.

The engagement took place at night, in the wildest kind of mêlée, the rival forces tangling in a confusion of flares, searchlights, gun flashes and burning ships. American vessels found themselves among Japanese craft and vice versa. In the darkness a commander might suddenly see himself in point-blank cannon range of a hostile ship. Sometimes Americans and Japs were almost alongside each other—and this was the case with the *Laffey*.

Lieutenant Commander Hank had his destroyer in the thickest of a swirl of battle. The small fast craft dashed ahead, looking for something that it might attack. Suddenly something loomed up, something huge—and it was Japanese. The destroyer was almost on top of an enemy monster. Dodge out of harm's way? Turn and try to escape? Not a bit. The American destroyer went right on.

Hank took the *Laffey* right under the nose of the Japanese battleship, and battered the sea giant at the closest range. The official communique states: "The *Laffey* passed so close under the bow of the speeding Japanese battleship that the range would have been point-blank with pea shooters."

Let's see how the Navy tells the story. The account, issued by the Twelfth Naval District at San Francisco, relates that the *Laffey*, the mere eighteen-hundred-ton destroyer, first engaged a small cruiser, knocked out the cruiser's searchlights and silenced its guns. Then came the colossal thing, which the Navy described in these words: "Out of the shadow of Guadalcanal came a Japanese battleship. The *Laffey* moved in as a terrier moves in on a grizzly, outweighed twenty to one."

The destroyer charged the battleship, and in a hail of fire let go a salvo of torpedoes. Two of them were seen to be direct hits.

The *Laffey* and the Japanese giant were so close together that the speed of the two ships carried them almost to a collision, the destroyer passing in front of the battleship.

"As the bows crossed," stated the Navy, "the Japanese on the forward deck could have tossed a hand grenade on the deck of the destroyer." At that range the *Laffey* turned all four of its five-inch guns against the Japanese monster. "The battleship's bridge," related the Navy account, "appeared literally to pulverize and blow away—it was shot completely off the ship." Here was the story of David and Goliath all over again.

The *Laffey*, speeding from under the bows of the battleship, ran on into another wild mêlée, mixing it with Japanese destroyers. She sank one. But another Japanese scored a torpedo hit. The *Laffey* got out of it, still on the surface but hopelessly battered and on fire. The crew abandoned ship. An internal explosion ripped the *Laffey* apart, and the little giant-killer plunged to the bottom of the southern ocean.

Captain Hank was still aboard when the *Laffey* blew up. He was never seen again: the Blue and the Gray going to hero graves together in the sea.

Skippers of the U.S.S. *Enterprise*. Commanding officers of the American aircraft carrier, which chalked up such a brilliant combat record in the Pacific, were: (upper left) Rear Admiral George D. Murray, U.S.N.; (upper right) Rear Admiral Arthur C. Davis, U.S.N.; (lower left) Rear Admiral Osborne B. Hardison, U.S.N.; (lower right) Captain Samuel P. Ginder, U.S.N.

Action in the Battle of Santa Cruz, October 26: A Japanese bomb splashes astern of the
U. S. carrier *Enterprise* as the enemy plane pulls out of its dive directly above the carrier.
The stormy sky is black-flecked with antiaircraft bursts; a destroyer can be seen astern of
the battleship; the cruiser from which the picture was taken leaves a curving white wake
as she turns in avoiding tactics.

THE WORK HORSE OF WAR

THE *Enterprise* was the first American aircraft carrier ever to
receive a Presidential citation, honor paid to the ship, the planes,
the crew: everything. The record of the flat-top, commanded by
Rear Admiral Kayley Davis, accounts amply for the distinction.
It also explains why they call the *Enterprise* the "Work Horse of
War."

The story begins on the fateful morning of December 7,
when the *Enterprise* was on her way to Pearl Harbor. It was
lucky for the carrier that she didn't get there sooner. If she had,
she might have been one of the ships in the harbor when the

Japanese planes came over and unloosed their hell of high explosive. Save for a bit of luck, the flat-top probably would have been either destroyed or disabled for some time to come. As it was, the *Enterprise* was out at sea. She sent her planes to Pearl Harbor, but the Japanese had already struck their sneak punch and were gone.

Thereafter the *Enterprise* was in nearly every engagement of the Pacific war. She was part of the task force that, little over a month after Pearl Harbor, launched America's first counter blow, the raid against the Marshall and Gilbert Islands. The *Enterprise* hurled eight separate plane attacks against Japanese positions on the island. Admiral Halsey, who commanded the task force, later stated: "The action embraced to the best of my knowledge the first instance in history of offensive combat by U. S. carriers. The performance of the *Enterprise* justifies the highest hopes heretofore held regarding the effectiveness of these vessels when properly employed."

The *Enterprise* was in the next two offensive blows launched against the Japanese, the raid on Wake Island, and the one that hit Marcus Island. And the flat-top was a member of the task force that carried the Doolittle bombers for the raid against Tokyo. The *Enterprise* protected the *Hornet*, aboard which the army bombers were placed. The big planes could be accommodated only on the deck, which was covered with them, so that the *Hornet* could not possibly have launched her own fighting planes if she were attacked. It's hard to think of anything more helpless than an aircraft carrier with a deckload of army bombers. The *Enterprise*, with her planes provided the air protection, ready to guard the *Hornet* against the Japanese, who, however, were too much surprised and disconcerted to try anything.

Captain Davis and his carrier missed the Battle of the Coral Sea. The *Enterprise*, which steamed from Pearl Harbor, arrived after the engagement was over. But the carrier was in the thick of things at Midway. Her planes made four separate attacks on the enemy invasion fleet. In one of these, thirty-three *Enterprise* dive bombers went after a Japanese force of four carriers, two battleships, four cruisers, and six destroyers. The big enemy flat-top

Members of an antiaircraft machine gun battery at battle stations after repelling a Japanese bomber in an attempted suicide plunge on the U.S.N. aircraft carrier *Enterprise*.

Kaga was hit squarely by eight bombs. The *Akagi* got three. These results of the one attack were sufficient to disable the two flat-tops, and left them a mark for subsequent bombing that day. Both sank, as did the flat-top *Soryu* that same day, when seventeen *Enterprise* dive bombers, reinforced by seven from another carrier, flashed out of the sun to blast the *Soryu* until the flat-top flamed from stem to stern and sank. On the second day at Midway the *Enterprise* scored five bomb hits on a big cruiser, and six fighting planes from the carrier sprayed two destroyers with machine-gun fire at point-blank range.

The height of drama and peril came in the sea and air battles of the Solomon Islands. The *Enterprise* started in by taking a major part in the beating off one of the first big Japanese attempts to reinforce the enemy troops on Guadalcanal. The carrier specialized in shooting down planes that day, running up a count of thirty. She also sank a submarine. The *Enterprise* was hit by air bombs and her crew was still repairing the damage when she got into her next big fight. It was the Battle of the Santa Cruz Islands, in which the *Hornet* was sunk. The Japs went out to get the *Enterprise* too. The carrier was hit and smashed up sufficiently to compel her to go to port for repairs; in two weeks she was back in action, grimly showing the scars of battle, but ready to lash out with savage blows through the air.

This the *Enterprise* did in that Solomon Island climax: the great naval battle of Guadalcanal. Nine torpedo planes from the carrier assailed a huge battleship of the *Kongo* class. The sea giant was protected by a heavy escort of cruisers and destroyers, but the torpedo planes of the *Enterprise* got through and scored three torpedo hits on the battleship. They returned to the carrier, loaded up with more ammunition, returned and smashed the battleship with three more torpedoes. When last seen, the Japanese monster was lying dead in the water. The next day *Enterprise* dive bombers repeatedly hit and probably sank a heavy cruiser, bombed a light cruiser, and damaged another heavy cruiser and a transport.

To summarize the work performed by the "Work Horse" mark down the following: She blasted enemy ships and shore installations with more than eighty-four thousand tons of bombs. She scored eleven torpedo hits, plus one probable torpedo hit. Her planes took part in the sinking of four aircraft carriers and three destroyers. They probably sank one battleship, one heavy cruiser, three large tankers, and a transport. The *Enterprise*, moreover, sank three submarines. The damage list includes direct hits on a carrier, a battleship, two light cruisers, and a destroyer, not counting smaller vessels. The havoc wrought by the *Enterprise* is estimated at from eight to ten times her original cost, and she's still going strong.

PART ELEVEN

ON TO NORTH AFRICA

CAPTAIN FREDERICK F. WESCHE 3RD, Roselle, New Jersey
Distinguished Service Cross
Flying Cross
Silver Star and Air Medal

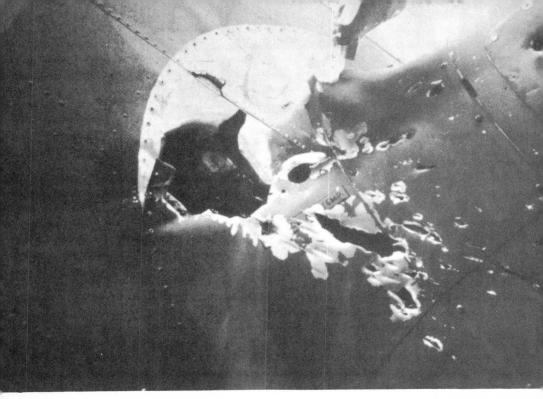

A Japanese antiaircraft shell hit Wesche's, "Flying Fortress" at the junction of wing and fuselage, and burst inside the plane. The shell burst set fires, but the Fortress got back to its base.

WITH THE FORTRESSES IN NEW GUINEA

"LOOK HERE," he began, "I didn't do anything more than plenty of the other fellows out in New Guinea, and I don't want to be singled out for anything exceptional. Many of the others did as much, or more."

"This book," I assured him, "is to be a description of representative Medal Men. They're simply to stand as examples of the whole group of Americans who have distinguished themselves."

"Okay," he answered.

The hero was Captain Frederick Wesche of Roselle, New Jersey, a star pilot of the Flying Fortresses based on New Guinea. His first decoration was conferred on him for a gallant attempt to save the life of General Walker, who was lost in an air battle with the Japanese.

When asked about that combat he said: "We took off from Port Moresby, a squadron of Flying Fortresses and Liberators," he related. "Our target was Rabaul, the powerful Japanese naval base in the Bismarck Archipelago. Rabaul is second only to Truk, the Japanese Pearl Harbor. General Walker rode in the lead plane, which was piloted by Major Bleasdale. We flew along in formation, until we got to Rabaul, and then broke formation to bomb.

"The antiaircraft fire was heavy and accurate. Many of the planes were hit. You should have seen some of the holes in the wings and the fuselages when we returned. A dozen Zeros or so went at us, but they didn't display any too much determination. Toward the end of the year out there, we noticed that the Zeros were growing less bold, and we figured that the Japanese pilots were not so good as they had been. They must have lost plenty of their picked men.

"We bombed ships in the harbor at Rabaul, and scored many hits. Then we started back, flying to renew our formation a few miles from the target. Fortresses, you know, fly as a tight squadron to beat off attack. General Walker's ship was the lead plane, and we looked for it so that we might form up behind it. But it was missing: we couldn't spot it anywhere.

"Then my tail gunner sang out that he had spied a Fortress in trouble behind us. I looked, and there it was off in the distance —trailing smoke. It was General Walker's plane. We never knew whether it had been hit by antiaircraft shell or shot up by Zeros, but it was on fire. The Zeros might not be so bold against an able-bodied bomber, but there was nothing they liked so well as to gang a crippled plane.

"The thing to do in a case like that was for the other Fortresses to form up around the damaged ship, and protect it, keeping it inside of the guns of the formation as long as it could fly. As quickly as possible I turned back toward the General's plane. The Zeros were thick, swarming around like flies, while we blazed away at them. As we drew closer to General Walker's ship, we could see that it had been badly hit, judging from the amount of smoke pouring out. Then it disappeared. The Fortress swept downward and into a bank of clouds. We never saw it again, and we figured it must have been forced down on the sea. The next day the Japanese announced that they had captured General Walker, which may or may not have been true."

Captain Wesche was decorated again for a thriller of night bombing off the northern coast of New Guinea, where the Japanese were trying to run re-enforcements to their be-leaguered garrisons at Lae and Salamau.

"We had them so well blockaded," he reported, "that they had given up trying to send convoys, and were resorting to fast trips by destroyers. These would dash in at night and unload drums of materials into the sea, in the hope that they would be picked up later by the Japanese on land. We called this kind of service the 'Tokyo Express' and we kept a vigilant air patrol—trying to get a crack at the destroyers.

"We were on patrol one night, and the water was pitch black. We couldn't see a thing. Suddenly one crew member sang out, 'There's a ship below.' Straining our eyes, we could sense, rather than clearly see, the ship. The position was near the shore, where it would be likely to drop supplies.

"Suddenly the ship, or ships as it turned out to be, below began to move. There were a number of them, but they had spotted us with their sound detectors probably, and did not want to be lying motionless on the water as the bombs descended all around them. Destroyers are so fast and so nimble that it is diffi-cult to hit them when they are dodging and twisting. We could now see the ships below clearly; that is, we could see their gleaming wakes. A moving ship leaves phosphorescent streams behind it, especially in the tropical waters.

"We picked out one of the destroyers, and went after it, flying at a low altitude of two thousand feet. We made several trial runs, to get the target lined up properly, and then three bombing runs. I was surprised the Jap did not open with searchlights and guns, because he certainly had us spotted. I suppose he did not want to give himself away with lights and gun flashes, until he thought he had us just where he wanted us. We scored a direct hit, as could be seen easily from the flash from the bomb. Then the Jap opened on us, the destroyer flaming with gunfire.

"I was working the controls, when a shattering detonation burst inside the plane. There's nothing quite so jarring and stunning as a shell exploding inside. The shell came in just at the junction of the wing and the fuselage, where it smashed a big hole. It was the kind of hit that might easily blast the wing off, but luckily, the plane held together. However, the explosion smashed a valve of the hydraulic system and set a fire of blazing oil. The electrical system was wrecked, and the lights on the instrument board went out. The engine control was hit, and one engine was put out. A mechanic standing close behind me was sprayed with shell fragments, just as if he were peppered with buckshot.

"We were badly damaged, and our plane was on fire, the crew fighting the blaze desperately. We lost altitude until we were flying at only five or six hundred feet above the water. We had only one bomb left but we could not drop it, because the explosion as it hit the ocean would have blown us up. One of the men disconnected the firing mechanism, and then we let the bomb go. We got the fire out, and headed for the nearest American flying field, which was at Buna. Although that was only a short distance away, we ran into a Japanese air raid. Field searchlights were combing the sky, as well as antiaircraft fire. If we, an unreported plane, had tried to go in, we would have been shot down. Instead, we turned out to sea and cruised around in the crippled plane. We might finally have been forced down out there, but luckily daybreak soon came. When it grew light, we flew into Buna for a crash landing."

The modest flyer who protested that there were many a lot of fellows out in New Guinea who had done as much as he, or had done more, was a member of the famous 19th Bombardment Group, which performed prodigies of valor against impossible odds in the Philippines during the first days of war and then was transferred to the Australian and New Guinea theatres.

Wesche joined the immortal outfit after its arrival in the Southwest Pacific, and promptly proved himself to be a better flyer, worthy of 19th Bombardment tradition. In one air engagement after another he added exploits of his own to that tradition. He did not want to be singled out in this book for anything he had done. So let us give the cheer to all the men of the 19th Bombardment Group.

CAPTAIN THOMAS L. GATCH, U.S.N., Annapolis, Maryland
Navy Cross

The way Japanese torpedo planes look as they approach an American warship: a picture of an attack that failed, the warship eluding the torpedoes. Captain Gatch's battleship survived three waves of attack by bombers and torpedo planes.

WHEN THE JAPANESE TRAPPED THEMSELVES

THE NAVAL BATTLE of Guadalcanal, in addition to the spectacular stroke launched by Admiral Callaghan's cruisers, had a battleship angle. A force of the American capital ships plus destroyers played a separate part in the great engagement. One battleship distinguished itself particularly in a daring night-fighting maneuver which resulted in a spectacular close-up slugging match with the enemy, and the skipper of the monster wrote his name, inscribed it with the flame of cannon fire on the roll of sea-fighting fame. He was Captain Thomas Leigh Gatch of Annapolis, Maryland.

[297]

There was one thing to be noted about the Captain—the arm that dangled uselessly at his side. He went into the Guadal-canal battle with an uncured shoulder injury from a previous scrap: lame arm, shoulder ripped and battered. Perhaps he should have been in the hospital instead of faring forth for battle again, but here's the story of how it happened.

The battleship had recently made its first appearance in the waters of the Solomons, its crew perfectly green so far as fighting went, straight from United States waters, fresh from eventless cruises and the makebelieve of maneuver. The big battlewagon was given a place in a task force moving toward the Japanese fleet, and was assigned to the job of protecting an aircraft carrier. The hostile naval squadrons approached each other, and Japanese planes spotted the battleship guarding the carrier. They swarmed to the attack, picking the battlewagon as their target. Perhaps they were thinking of how Japanese air power had bombed, torpedoed, and sunk the mighty British capital ships, the *Prince of Wales* and the *Repulse*, and were out to emulate that exploit by sinking an American battleship. At any rate, they tried hard. There were three consecutive air attacks by powerful forces of bombers and torpedo planes. These were beaten off with heavy losses, but the battleship sus-tained one dramatic hit.

The first enemy wave consisted of twenty dive bombers. All were shot down by the antiaircraft guns of the battlewagon, which did some fast maneuvering to evade the high explosive. These gyrations worried Captain Gatch. "Our ship," he said later, "was cutting circles and figure eights and other maneuvers without names. I was more afraid of ramming the carrier than of the attacking planes."

In the second attack forty torpedo planes and dive bombers swung to the assault. Antiaircraft fire beat them off and shot them down. Only one got through, a torpedo plane. Its deadly missile, designed to cut through the water, hopped over the battleship, jumped over the deck, the tin fish behaving like a flying fish. That seems fantastic, but here's how it happened.

Telling how the attacking plane came straight at the battleship, speeding toward the stern, Captain Gatch relates: "It appeared that millions of tracer shells went right past that plane without hitting it. But some did strike it—and at the right time. They struck just before the pilot released his torpedo. The plane was jarred out of its line of flight, and its torpedo was released while up in the air. It seemed as if the torpedo would drop on the ship, but it passed over the fantail and fell into the sea on the other side aft." So that's how a torpedo sailed over a battleship. "The plane's wings were shot off," adds Captain Gatch. "It struck the water and sank."

In the third attack the battleship was hit. Twenty-four torpedo planes and dive bombers swarmed to the assault, and one Jap pilot discharged his bomb with accurate aim.

"I was out on the catwalk in front of the bridge, where I had no business to be," Captain Gatch reports. "The bridge was protected. I was out in the open to get a better look at the enemy planes. I was in that exposed position when the dive bomber got in its blow.

"I saw its bomb released from not more than one hundred feet above the forward part of the ship." He goes on to say he hoped the bomb would strike a turret and not the deck. It was a good-size bomb, probably a five-hundred-pounder, and it might blow a hole in the deck and kill the crew members beneath. Certainly it would kill many in the gun crews on the deck itself. "The automatic guns forward," adds the Captain, "were manned by mess attendants, some Filipinos, some Negroes. They never stopped firing for a second: those men were good."

The Captain's wish was fulfilled. The bomb did not strike the deck where its blast would have smashed men of the crew. It hit the turret, where its explosion could hit only the Captain. In the frightful explosion a fragment of the bomb slashed his neck, severing an artery. The force of the blast hurled him against the conning tower, and knocked him out. The muscles of his shoulder were badly ripped.

They picked him up, unconscious and bleeding, stopped the blood flow from the severed neck artery, and brought him back to consciousness. The shoulder and arm were permanently injured. In the hospital he recovered from his other wounds, but his arm hung limp. He felt ready for another fight, however. The Admiral in command said okay, in spite of the arm.

"I don't expect you to strangle Japs," commented the Admiral.

So it was that Captain Gatch, lame arm and all, took his battleship into that spectacular night engagement at sea called the Battle of Guadalcanal.

There is a narrow strait between Guadalcanal and the adjacent island of Savo, a blustery stretch of water where the sea winds roar. American seamen called it *Windy Gulch*. Captain Gatch's battleship with other ships passed through Windy Gulch. But, outside the winds, there was nothing stirring, not a sign of enemy action. Yet they had reason to suspect that the Japanese were lying in wait.

"They had set a trap," relates the Captain, "and we were trying to find it—so we could go in it and get caught. We wanted to get caught. They weren't expecting us. They had set this trap for foxes, and we didn't think it would hold bear." In other words, the Japs had laid a snare for light craft and were embarrassed to catch battleships instead.

Enemy ships suddenly loomed out of the night—three cruisers, a large one and two small ones. The sixteen-inch guns of the American warships opened up at a range of only several miles, and the night was dispersed when the leading cruiser, the big one, burst into flames. The towering blaze clearly showed up the other cruisers behind her. All three were sunk before their own smaller guns got within range of the mightily armed battleship—before they could even see the battleship. Star shells which they fired in the general direction of the big American battlewagon fell thousands of yards short. "They never knew just what sank them," says Captain Gatch.

Then, after that mishap to their cruisers, the Japanese let go with their already badly sprung trap. This occurred when the American force passed north of Savo Island and turned south. The ships were now in a passage with constricted channels and many shoals, a bad spot for a battleship, making quick maneuvering impossible. An enemy ship—a big destroyer or large cruiser—appeared. Three salvos from the battleship's turret guns, and the Jap burst into flames and sank stern first.

Enemy cruisers and destroyers were lined up in ambush alongside the cliffs of Savo Island, where it was impossible to spot them from the air. They were here hidden to deliver a surprise torpedo attack against anything going through the passage. The American force was led by destroyers, and these were the target for the blow launched from the Jap hiding place under the shelter of the cliffs, cruisers and destroyers lashing out for a torpedo attack. They were unaware that battleships were behind the destroyers—not until four searchlights from a Japanese cruiser picked out Captain Gatch's giant ship.

"Within a second after the searchlights were on us," the Captain relates, "our secondary batteries opened up, and their searchlights went out. Thirty seconds later our main batteries tired."

The battleship was engaged with the cruiser when a Japanese battleship joined the fray. Another American battleship went after the Jap, smashing it with shellfire. A shell from one of the Jap cruisers scored a hit on the conning tower of Captain Gatch's battleship, and this started a fire which blazed like a beacon at the top of the conning tower.

"I was on the catwalk," the Captain relates. "I had been dying for a cigarette and now I thought I'd have one. So I drew my lighter. One of the men shouted, 'Captain, sir! You'll give away our position.' I just looked at the flames up near the top of our mast," says the Captain, "and finished the cigarette." An ironical episode of naval battle—flames glaring in the night at the top of the tall conning tower, blazing like a huge torch, and a sailor warning the commander that a light from a cigarette would give away the position of the ship.

The Captain had his smoke while the fire was being extinguished. The fight was soon over.

In the Battle of Guadalcanal the Japanese baited a trap for rabbit and got bear; the American capital ships were grizzlies that the Japs could not learn to handle.

LIEUTENANT GENERAL MARK W. CLARK, INFANTRY, Madison Barracks, New York
Purple Heart
Distinguished Service Medal

The North African offensive, American troops going ashore in landing barges. You can see the excitement in the faces of the two men, as United States forces seize the port of Fedala in French Morocco. The offensive was such a great success largely because of General Clark's adventure of negotiation—a message to Garcia.

WHO SAID "MESSAGE TO GARCIA"?

THEY LIKENED General Clark's adventure to that famous "Message to Garcia," Elbert Hubbard's tale of an American officer in the Spanish-American War who went on a mission to a Cuban insurgent named Garcia. The Elbert Hubbard story is said to have sold a hundred million copies. But the "Message to Garcia" was tame beside General Mark W. Clark's secret mission.

While the Allied North African offensive was in preparation, a group of high French officers in North Africa made a rather good guess of what was coming. Though in the service of the Vichy Government, they were anti-Nazi and secretly favored the cause of the United Nations. Among them were representatives of General Giraud, the French officer who had made two dramatic escapes from Germany. Giraud, in Vichy-controlled France, wanted to join in some action against the Nazis, and through representatives in Africa inquired about the possibilities.

The group of patriotic Frenchmen got in touch with American representatives, and suggested that an American general be sent secretly to meet them at Algiers. This word was transmitted to the War Department in Washington where it was okayed.

As the man to lead the undercover mission, the War Department selected Major General Mark W. Clark—forty-six years old, slim and sharp-eyed, an able soldier and an astute diplomat. He got in contact with the French officers with whom negotiations were to be conducted, and arranged a trip to meet them—a trip that would make the thrills of a mystery novel seem pale. Much of the story of how they got to Africa and met the French officers is still a military secret. Later, when the Allies invaded North Africa, General Clark said: "I used planes, trains, ships, submarines, canoes, automobiles—everything but mules."

The high spot of the expedition came when the Clark mission finally made its way to Algiers. It had been arranged that when they got to a certain point along the Algerian coast, a signal—a light in the window of a certain house—would be flashed to them.

When they arrived on the prearranged night, however, the signal failed to come. What was wrong? General Clark and his companions were afraid they had been led into a trap. They waited until the next night, kept in hiding, subsisting on the food they had brought with them. Late the next night, as they kept their eyes glued on the house, a flash suddenly pierced the darkness, a lighted window as though a curtain had been raised. They went up to the house, which was shrouded in darkness except for the signal window. The owner of the house came out to greet them. He told them that they were perfectly safe, that in order to preserve secrecy he had sent his wife away, also his Arab servants, giving them a few days off.

The Americans were led inside. "The house," General Clark

relates, "was filled with French military officers in uniform—although they had come to the place in civilian clothes." They had journeyed to the rendezvous in civilian clothes for secrecy, but wore their uniforms during the conference to give it a more official status.

"We conferred all day and all night, until we had gathered all the information we wanted," says General Clark. That information was plenty—and vital.

The French officers agreed to collaborate with the forthcoming American offensive. They gave the Americans complete plans of all French military installations in North Africa, the disposition of troops, the type of equipment and garrisons, and data as to which French leaders could be counted friendly. They even made an arrangement to have the airfields outside Algiers delivered over to General Jimmy Doolittle's air force, once the offensive began.

An agreement was made with representatives of General Giraud. "In this conference, Clark opened negotiations which brought about the collaboration of Giraud with the United Nations," states the War Department in Washington.

Adding it all up—the secret mission headed by General Clark laid all the important groundwork for the invasion of French North Africa.

The conference was a complete success—and then came a break of bad luck that almost resulted in the ruin of the whole offensive. The secret meeting was nearly discovered, the Americans were within a hairbreadth of being detected and arrested by the Vichy authorities.

The Arab house servants who had been given several days off grew suspicious. They went to the Vichy police and tipped them off about the suspicious house. Luckily there were anti-Nazi elements among the police, and the conference was just being completed when word came that the police were on their way.

"I never saw such excitement in my life," laughs General Clark. "Maps disappeared like lightning. A French General in military uniform changed into civilian clothes in one minute flat. I last saw him going out of a window."

General Clark and his group of Americans gathered their papers—the vital information that had been given to them. They ducked down into an empty wine cellar. Hiding there, they could hear the arrival of the police, and the talk between the Vichy henchmen and the owner of the house.

As they crouched in the darkness, one of the officers was seized with an almost uncontrollable desire to cough. "I am afraid," he whispered, "that if I hold this cough back any longer, I am going to choke to death."

They expected that at any minute the police would come down into the cellar. General Clark crouched with his revolver in his hand. "If the police came down," he relates, "I was undecided whether to shoot them or bribe them. I had fifteen thousand francs in my pocket."

But the Vichy police did not think about the cellar, and after hanging around for an hour, and finding nothing out of the way, they left.

The Americans were able to leave the house. They went to the shore where small boats awaited them, climbed aboard and started to leave Africa behind them. But—the straw that broke the camel's back—the surf was too strong, the boats capsized, and the whole group was thrown into the water. Most of the men lost their clothes, and General Clark his trousers, but that wasn't all. "I lost some eighteen thousand dollars in gold," said the General afterward. Then he laughed: "I wonder if Morgenthau will get after me for that."

But they managed to save their papers—the invaluable data for the great offensive. They got ashore and, in their underclothes, hid all day in a patch of woods, cold and shivering. At long last, pro-Allied agents got in touch with them, and they were taken out of North Africa—to report back home with their vital information.

Later, after the offensive had been launched with such pronounced success, American Commander General Eisenhower summarized the accomplishments of General Clark: "The fact that land resistance was not terrifically great anywhere and that we did not have to land any place where opposition was great—

testifies to the success of the Clark mission.' And the General added, "It was a modern 'Message to Garcia.'"

The North African offensive issued in a new phase of America's war, the direct battle against the Nazis. The landings in the French colonies were made in November, toward the end of our first year in the global conflict. The second year of our war opened with the blast of guns and the rumbling of tanks in Tunisia. But that's another story.

Our effort in the first twelve months of war was mostly in the Pacific. After Pearl Harbor came the series of sea and air raids against the Japs, then the battles of Coral Sea, Midway, and the Solomon Islands. The first year was predominantly an affair of the Pacific. It was one phase of our fight with Japan, and it was completed—to be renewed later when the time comes to smite the Jap with everything we have, the prelude to final victory. As the year ended the focus of war shifted all the way around the world to the Mediterranean theatre. The phrase "global war" is right.

What will be the issue of the events that have begun with the second year, the year of emphasis on Africa, the Mediterranean, Europe? What ultimate results will proceed from the great North African victory, the bombing of Italy and Germany, the plans for an invasion of the Nazi European stronghold, the Roosevelt-Churchill determination to crush Hitler? To this aspect of history in the making we now turn our thoughts, after having surveyed the first year, with its accent on the Pacific, surveyed it in terms of its heroes.

ACKNOWLEDGMENTS

The photographs noted below have been approved by the Bureau of Public Relations, War Department, Washington, D. C., and credit is due to the following sources:

U. S. Navy: Pages 2, 3, 7, 10, 11, 15, 19, 33, 37, 52, 53, 60, 64, 65, 72, 77, 81, 84, 85, 90, 91, 94, 98, 99, 107, 120, 121, 124, 125, 128, 129, 134, 135, 141, 144, 145, 146, 148, 149, 152, 156, 157, 160, 161, 167, 171, 174, 175, 178, 179, 184, 185, 207, 225, 229, 240, 241, 246, 247, 250, 251, 254, 255, 258, 259, 262, 263, 268, 269, 271, 276, 277, 280, 284, 285, 287, 297, 303.

U. S. Marine Corps: Pages 14, 18, 166, 170, 188, 189, 191, 196, 197, 202, 203, 206, 213, 220, 221, 224, 228.
U. S. Army Signal Corps: Pages 40, 43, 46, 47, 56, 57, 69, 302.
U. S. Army Air Forces: Pages 24, 32, 36, 102, 103, 106, 114.
U. S. Coast Guard: Pages 73, 210, 211, 212.

Credit is also due to the following for use of photographs in this book:

Acme: Pages 25, 29, 61.
Press Association: Pages 6, 153, 236.
Wide World: Pages 28, 76.
Harris & Ewing: Page 68.
Movietone: Page 115